Morelle Smith's poetry, fiction and journalism has appeared in both print and online journals and anthologies, such as *Scottish Review*, *Times Literary Supplement*, *La Traductière*, *Ljubljana Tales*, *New Eastern Europe*, *Balkan Traveller*s etc. She has lived and worked in Germany, France and Albania and her travels have taken her across the USA, Europe and Asia. She has won prizes and awards for her writing, including the Audience Award for her poetry in Kyiv, Ukraine (2014). Her most recent books are the travel memoir *Tirana Papers* (Kairos, Edinburgh, 2013) and the poetry collection *The Definition of Happiness* (Bibliotheca Universalis, Bucharest, 2015).

Her blog is http://rivertrain.blogspot.co.uk

CW01560502

Also by Morelle Smith

The Star Reaper (Grade One Press, Edinburgh, 1980)
Deepwater Terminal (diehard, Edinburgh, 1998)
Streets of Tirana, Almost Spring (Ora Publishing, Albania, 2004)
The Way Words Travel (UKA Press, Bristol, 2005)
The Ravens and the Lemon Tree (diehard, Callander, 2008)
Time Loop (Playback Editions, Shetland, 2010)
Gold Tracks, Fallen Fruit (Cestrian Press, Chester, 2011)
Tirana Papers (Kairos, Edinburgh, 2013)
The Definition of Happiness (Bibliotheca Universalis, Bucharest, 2015)

Every Shade of Blue

Morelle Smith

Kairos

First published 2013 by Kairos
20 Fleming Place
Fountainhall
TD1 2TA

ISBN: 978-0-9927233-3-0

Printed in the UK by Bell & Bain Ltd., Glasgow

The paper used in this book is recyclable. It is made from low chlorine pulps produced in a low energy, low emissions manner from renewable forests.

Typeset and design by Main Point Books, Edinburgh
www.mainpointbooksco.uk

For John Renbourn (1944–2015)

Acknowledgements

'Texas Night' was first published in *Deep Water Terminal* (diehard, 1998); 'Remembering Giancarlo' first appeared in *The Way Words Travel* (UKA Press, 2005); and the excerpt from 'Clusone' was first published in *Sons of Camus Writers International Journal* (2006). Thanks are due to the editors and publishers.

I am grateful to Dave Goulder for permission to quote from 'From Sandwood down to Kyle'.

Contents

Blue was John Renbourn's favourite colour. From his clothes, to his pottery – cups, plates, teapots – to the waxed tablecloth bought at a small French market, to the views out over European seas – the Adriatic, Ionian, the Mediterranean.

During the 1990s, I accompanied John on some of his tours of Europe and the USA. Written in planes, cars, ferries, cafés and hotel rooms, these journals are an assortment of stories, conversations, landscapes and flights of imagination.

The scenery, just like the music, changed mood and tempo. Some places were erased from immediate memory, obscured sometimes by lack of sleep and sometimes because there was no time for impressions to be assimilated, before we had to leave for the next gig, the next flight, the next journey by car, the next town. Some places, for no obvious reason, stood out with startling clarity. And the music was always the backdrop.

But the journey began at a leisurely pace, in France, on a cold day in February 1995. We were heading south from Paris to the Languedoc, taking the scenic route to a village near Albi where John would give a concert with the Bosnian cellist Vedran Smailović.

Every Shade of Blue

John Renbourn at rue Guillaume de Machault, Reims, France

John Renbourn at Duddo stone circle, Northumberland, England

I

Cathar Country

Our first stop was a visit to friends, Dominique and Brigitte, who live near Paris. We all went for a meal at a Vietnamese restaurant and Dom insisted that afterwards, we try a drink with an unmemorable name. He and Brigitte started laughing and said that it was a very amusing drink. I tried to pass on this as I'd had plenty of red wine, but it turned out that no was not an option, this drink had to be experienced. The waiter brought a jug and four little cups. He placed a cup in front of each of us and then changed his mind, put John's cup in front of me and mine in front of John as if it mattered who got which cup.

Why did he do that? I asked.

You will see, said Dom mysteriously.

The little cups were like thimbles that had been washed too often and were stretched out of shape. As the drinks were poured from jug to cups, the jug whistled softly to itself. Once the liquid was in, a miniature picture of a naked man appeared on the bottom of my cup. I didn't know how this magic worked but Dom says it was something to do with reflection. When the thimble cup was empty the vision disappeared and to make it reappear, you had to pour more of the liquid into the cup. The men get an image of a naked woman, which is why it was important for each person to get the 'right' cup.

Our intention was to leave fairly early the next morning. Dominique and Brigitte had already gone out to visit some friends. I was downstairs in the kitchen, making coffee, when I heard a cracking and thumping noise from upstairs, followed by a yell. As I went to investigate I heard slightly hiccupy noises but it was difficult to know if the sounds were of distress or of helpless laughter. On arrival at the scene, I discovered it was the latter. After having a shower John had decided to return to bed for a short rest while waiting for the coffee to be brewed. In a fit of enthusiasm he'd flung himself onto the bed, which had broken and tipped him onto the floor.

This is serious, he said through gasps of laughter – this is not my bed and I'm going to have to fix it.

But he just happened to have a tool kit in the car, so he went to fetch a hammer.

Very flimsily made he muttered, as he hammered the wooden bed-boards together. Without the small broken piece that connected side and end-boards I did not really know how he managed to repair it but after testing it very carefully, the bed held together.

After toast and coffee we made a quick and guilty exit. Our first stop was at the nearby garage, to fill the car with petrol, before the drive south.

I should have paid more attention, I really should. But somehow I thought that, with all John's experience of driving in Europe, he knew what he was doing and was perfectly capable of putting petrol in the car. He unlocked the cap, pulled out the metal nozzle, placed it in the petrol tank, pressed the lever and when the tank was full, he replaced it in its socket and went to the kiosk to pay. I'd consulted the map and discovered what road would take us south. And so we set off. But we had hardly gone a few meters before the engine began to cough, which turned into a fit and then it just gave up and died.

We looked at each other in consternation. We got out. Pushed the car to the side of the road.

Could it be? he murmured.

Something wrong with the petrol? I asked. Water in the tank?

There were different kinds of petrol at the garage. Maybe I chose the wrong one – *gazole* – something flickered at the back of my mind. Wasn't *gazole* –

Diesel?

Does this car run on diesel?

Uh – no. Petrol. Usually.

Saint Benoît du Sault – Limoges

So we spent another night chez Dom and Brigitte. As it was a Sunday, the car could not be repaired that day, but it had been towed back to the garage ready for the necessary draining and cleaning of the engine to take place the following morning. We left Dominique and Brigitte's early, to go and pick up the car. Before we left, Brigitte produced one of those battery operated crumb-eaters and proceeded to de-crumb the table and the floor round about. We watched this process with fascination, neither of us having encountered such a gadget before.

We speak franglais, fringlish and fronsense. We make up our own fax language, a special code, so no-one else can understand. Its basic binary premise is 'gap' and 'no gap', these being the two ends of extremes. Tea and chocolate hazelnut spread are at the plus end of the spectrum (no gap) along with Chartres Cathedral and mazes. Gazole and misleading maps (though not the map reader) are at the 'gap' end. The

Green Man, La Dame à la Licorne, the Pont Neuf, Sidi Brahim wine, Edith Piaf and Jean Cocteau are also at the 'no gap' end, especially if the latter two are sitting underneath a piano. This is because we found a postcard of them doing just that. We speculated as to why they were sitting under a piano, clearly carrying on an animated conversation. Perhaps the café or night club was crowded and there was nowhere else to sit. Perhaps they were moving the piano and were waiting for others to come and help and it had started to rain.

We stopped in Saint Benoît du Sault and bought bread, paté and cheese which we ate in the car. The crusty French bread left lots of crumbs on the car seat.

Look at all these crumbs, says I.

It's all right, I've got a crumb picker-upper, says John.

Did you get that in France or England?

Oh, I always carry one with me, wherever I go.

We stayed the night near Limoges at the Oak Tree Dawn (*L'Orée des Chênes*) then continued on the road south. It rained and rained. The road was lined with hedgerows and lots of pale-barked silver birches. There was gorse and whin and houses with red and cream tiles and soft green dollops of fur, ice-cream tiles, *profiteroles* rooftops.

When I was driving, John sharpened a pencil, and jotted down notes in the music notebook he bought in Champigny-sur-Marne, while we were waiting for the car to be cleaned. The smell of wood and lead from a sharpened pencil. Wipers beating against the windscreen and when we reached the motorway that circles round Toulouse, the big trucks threw mist and splashy waves of air behind them and I could hardly see a thing when I was overtaking.

When we reached Foix, we found a room in the hotel

Lons which looks out onto the river. I listened to John trying out the new tune he wrote as we were travelling. When he paused, there was the sound of the river.

Foix

When we woke up it was the first thing we heard, the sound of the Ariège river flowing just beneath the window. After breakfast we went exploring through the narrow streets, to the castle. Red rooftops were splashed below us, at all different angles and levels. There was the yellow stone cathedral and the castle with a round tower and a square tower and both had wooden spiral steps. The very bottom spiral was stone, with a dip in the middle, worn away by the passage of centuries of feet.

There were huge metal bolts on the wooden doors, as well

as padlocks. A drifting chain was lying idly against one door. A couple of the doors had peep-holes, where you could slide back a piece of wood and look in. Apparently, it was used as a prison for a while. Even the peep-hole shutters had massive ironmongery attached which would not shift when I tried to move them.

From the tower-tops there's a panoramic view over to the Pyrenees, which are topped with snow. There are little wispy bits of mist, lost straggles of cloud, irretrievably separated from the loose-weave of the light-grey, dark-grey, sky rug.

We drive east. The road climbs, the sky grows more uniformly, deeply grey. There's an occasional pine tree, flickers of almond blossom. We climb higher. There are pinnacles of rock fingers on the left. And the rain's going soft on us.

Roquefixade.

We walk up to the castle at Roquefixade, the rain turning to snow, the silence, stony low-sky silence, one wide-winged bird appearing, circling, disappearing, lumps of snow slipping off the trees, the mist moving in and we climb to the top, where the castle ruins rise above a sheer drop, rock-steep drop, all tall and thin and perpendicular, drop down, way down below into the valley.

On the way up John tells me about an accident he was involved in several years ago, where he lost his kneecap. Without a kneecap, bending one's knees in the way we do unthinkingly, is just not possible. I begin to understand why he's not so hot on his hooves. I tell him about the accident to my left knee – not nearly so debilitating, but still leaving a hefty scar – and we decide to form a left knee club. But I'm secretly very relieved when we are safely back down and I tell him we are not – well, he is not anyway – going to climb up to Monségur. Which is where we are headed. I'd first seen it a few years before, in high summer. I was also writing a novel, with Monségur as the focal point. So I justified – at least to myself – taking time off to go on this trip, as further research.

On a clear day, Monségur is visible from Roquefixade, but the day was far from clear, with the sleety mist drifting almost as far as the valley floor as we drove back downhill. Following the signs, the road started to climb again. It became steeper and twisting as it led to the foot of the spur of rock, pointing up to the sky. The castle of Monségur is perched on the top of this rocky spur. And as the car climbs, my excitement rises. But when we've gone as far as the car can go, the mist had not dispersed and the mountain was invisible, completely obscured in swirling, freezing mist. I got out of the car stunned, disbelieving. But there it was, a faint grey area marking the beginning of the mountain, and nothing above it but a fierce wrapping of protective mist.

John thinks it's funny but I feel subdued and reluctant to leave this place, looking back every so often just in case the mist was playing a trick on us and had suddenly lifted. But it did not, it followed us back down into the valley before it finally dispersed, to reveal the golden afternoon sunlight and long shadows painting the hills. The utter beauty of the landscape could not fail to lift my spirits, making me more philosophical and accepting of the rebuff, so I felt it to be, by the guardian gods of Monségur.

We pass Lavelanet and Quillan and go on to Rennes-les-Bains, shrouded in the shadows of deep green mountains. I'd been given an address here by a friend, but though we find the house, there is no-one at home. We visit the local café and I ask the lady there if she knows of a good place for us to stay the night. She tells us to go back down to Quillan and at the *feu rouge, tout droit, puis à droite*, and we'll find a château which lets out rooms. We follow her directions and there it is, a wonderful old building. We walk into a huge courtyard and climb spiral stone steps. In the courtyard three men are turning a large chunk of pig on a spit. Or that what it looks like to me. John says they're probably fixing a bit of a car but how he turns a pig's thigh into a car battery is beyond me.

I make one more attempt to get in touch with my friend in Rennes-les-Bains. There is a phone booth just off the courtyard, and I stumbled around in the dark, trying to read the creased bit of paper and the phone dials, not very successfully. The limping retainer with the twangy Midi accent took pity on me and went off to find something to illuminate the phone room. He came back later with a torch and a key, unlocked another door and turned on the light. This unexpected visibility was certainly a bonus and I succeeded in dialling the number. But there was no reply. I switched off the light and went back outside into the deserted courtyard. The thick silence settled around me. I lingered for a while, watching the deep black sky and Orion and Sirius cresting the horizon above the inky courtyard.

Montredon-Labessonier

«*Je porte gravé sur mon front*
L'image de la vérité de l'amour
Sûr qu'avec le temps j'arriverai là
ou l'on me comprendra même si
je ne parle pas.»— T. Campanella

Castel Frank, near Réalmont, newly acquired by the Dandelion Trust, is a large cold building, in the process of being renovated. Last night we ate in the huge main room, with a log fire in the vast fireplace, but it was still cold. Tonight it is a little warmer because of the many people who have come to hear the concert. John is playing and so is Vedran Smailović, the Bosnian cellist.

I am downstairs, in the kitchen. I am making a cup of tea. This is very special, to find tea. Everyone is milling around upstairs. We picked up Vedran and Amira from the train station at Carcassonne. We went for a drink before driving back to Montredon-Labessonier. Vedran is a large, large person, extravagant, extrovert, extra, extraordinary. The beer, the laughter, the big gestures, the wideness. Amira wrote down the lines by T. Campanella, in my notebook. Something about you brought those lines to mind, she said.

We head back to Castel Frank. I am driving and Vedran is sitting in the front passenger seat, John and Amira in the back. Vedran puts on a cassette of him playing the cello in the bombed city of Sarajevo. Shells dropping around him. I am close to tears.

The rain is hard, heavy, sweeping, buffeting the car. There is a bend in the road, to the left. An opening on the right. A car pulls out. It should not. I am on the main road, I have the right of way. But the car pulls out. Too close, it's too close, it's right in front of me on the road and it should not be. I try to pull to the right to avoid it, and brake. A bang, shock. The tape plays slow, it does not sound right, it whines, sounds terrible, that's what I think, that tape sounds awful. I do not want to look beside me, in case Vedran and the whole side of the car is mangled or missing.

But when I do look, he's still sitting there, quite intact.

Everyone is all right, everything's fine, they say.

I'm drinking a cup of Earl Grey tea in the huge kitchen of Castel Frank. Everything is fine.

*

Crossing the mountains of the Massif Central, from Espal-
ion to Aumont and then to Aubrac. There was rain and then
wind and hail, in gusts so fierce I could not see, even with the
wipers on full. Then the wind calmed a little and it turned
to snow. The little car lost power, going over these mountain passes. Sky all glowery angry, grey and gusting, wind
blowing snow onto the windscreen, snow on the road, then
little rivers crossing it, ponds, little lakes, hardly another car
passing us, going the other way.

Leaving the mountains behind, on the main road towards
Clermont-Ferrand the sun shows a little of its face, just a
rough and tumbled smile, glinting fragments of melody,

*"I met a man upon the road
and asked for charity"*

while the clouds sound a gentle background bass line.

At the entrance to Castel Frank there was a lodge house,
somewhat derelict and dilapidated, clearly unoccupied for
years. This was the sleeping quarters for some of the guests,
including us. There was an ancient stove, a kettle and a couple of mugs, one large armchair whose stuffing was coming
out, a wooden stool, and a few mattresses in the upstairs
rooms. It had the chill of old stone houses which have been
empty for years, and there was no heating. Yet it had its own
charm, with its deep-set windows and view out over waving
poplar trees. But it was a long avenue from the lodge house
to the château, and after the concert we drove slowly back
from the château to the entrance. The recent torrential rain
had turned the driveway into a combination of river deltas
and debris, bordered by deep mud. John said – one thing
for sure, we don't want to get stuck here, and as if on cue,

the moment he said the word 'stuck' the car slid gently off the track into the mud *et tous les chevaux du roi et tous les hommes du roi ne peuvent pas la remontre sur le chantier.*

Well, not quite true. *Le roi même ne peut pas le faire*, so he gave up, went to the lodge house, *boire du rouge, boire pour oublier ce jour trop, trop de tous, trop de conduire, trop d'accidents, trop de gendarmes* – so, I go to fetch the king's men and they push and heave the car, while I get behind the wheel and steer it back onto the track. Back on the track, back on the path.

Going over the mountains, we pass a sign for falling rocks. What might that mystic symbol mean? enquires He of the Dutch naval cap, recently acquired in Albi.

It's a sign for the duality of life, say I of the black beret, also acquired in Albi. You see where it says above it *'rappel'*, that's to remind us that we are but brief sojourners in this world of time and space, in the world but not of it, to remind us, always, of our spiritual nature.

Good, says he, but speaking of time, when we go to heaven together, we must not forget the sandwiches, the flask, the Nutella and the stolen Ricard ashtray.

Snow-covered mountains in the distance. Two coffees, large ones, with milk and sugar, in late afternoon. It's nearly 5 o'clock and Clermont-Ferrand still a hundred kilometres away and then we still have to get to Calais and then up the bleak corridor *anglaise*, to the Tron in Edinburgh, where Stewart and Shirley are playing tomorrow evening. Will we make it by then? Who can tell?

In front of us the sky is grimbely crushed green, crushed and squeezed and smoothed out, pale water-green wash and mashy clouds, in fluffed-up finery dancing across sky-stage.

'Use your engine braking' says the sign.

The side mirror, which used to swing in the wind like a weathervane, is now empty of mirror and the metal socket is jammed into the bonnet like an axe-head, the result of yesterday's accident. Now both front doors do not work properly. It used just to be the driver's one, which John mangled a bit after some whisky drinking up north, so there was difficulty in getting into it, but before I drove I just thought he had problems getting in, you know, people have their very individual problems, but I found it was mine too, when I got in that side. Well, since yesterday's short encounter with a white French car, the other front door also does not open properly, so now we have a matching set. Whichever side you get in now, you have to shrink yourself a little, fold yourself a little, and squeeze in.

*

Just south of Birmingham I check the car clock and discover that twenty-five and a half hours ago we left Castel Frank in the slightly misty early morning, while everyone else was still asleep. John did most of the driving after it got dark, while I dozed. We both fell asleep on the ferry from Calais to Dover.

And now the sun is shining, hazed by our half-dreaming half-awake state. *Entre le rêve et le retour.* It feels colder here, a different kind of cold, a more penetrating cold, *un froid intime.* The cathedral at Albi also has a quality of intimacy, with its ceiling and walls painted all over with colourful designs and figures. Not an inch of stone is left bare. It's vast yes, but perhaps it is the painted stone that gives it a touch of the personal, the intimate. Chartres cathedral is breathtaking and you tiptoe round it, slightly awestruck, slightly as if you are visiting someone else's place, and your presence is tolerated but not especially welcomed. But Albi's cathedral draws you in as if there is room for you, you have a place there, as if you are invited.

We drive on the flyover above the rooftops of Birmingham. Angled tower-blocks and squat pylons. When I close my eyes I see the road rolling in front of me. But I also see narrow French streets with yellowstone red-roofed houses, a road curving through villages of ancient buildings, their stone façades criss-crossed with thick timber black with age.

2

Yorkshire Dales

We begin the day with a view of broken windows, a derelict clump of red-brick buildings, all empty, all window-sculptured, sharp angles of dark with no reflections, then arrows of light-reflecting pane-pieces, showing you how dark buildings really are inside. How dark the earth is, under the canopy of cloud. Looking down on it from the air, from above the clouds, how dark to go in there, how light-bereaved, how weighed down.

We begin the day with reflections, in the shapes of the pointy kind of light you get from stars in children's drawings – and mine, because I have never achieved sophistication in drawing. I think this means trying to draw things as they really are, but I don't know how things really look, I only know how they look to me and that is always a mixture of them and me, a mixture of what I bring to it as well as what it brings to me. What I bring depends on how much sunlight there is, how much rain there is in the wind, how much memory, how many poplar trees line the roadsides and where I might sleep tonight.

Yesterday the Dales were snow-covered and when we stopped to drink the treacle tea made by *le roi lui-même,*

there was this view down into the valley, all snow-bandaged, crisp cotton wrappings, shrinking and fraying at edges. Well, there it was, looking nothing like the valley we overlooked near Rennes-les-Bains. That one had earth so red it was like crumbled bricks, a scarlet sand. *Le roi* drove the car to the edge of a precipice, so you could see nothing beneath you except this falling-away ground, falling into trees and red earth and in the distance, the hills were pale blue.

They really are blue, I said and we settled down to eat the croissants we'd bought in a village we'd passed through where everything was closed or *à vendre*, except for the *boulangerie* and there were these two croissants waiting for us. Chopped nuts on top, jam and spicy cake inside, we will – obviously – never taste their like again and if we ever do find that village again, the *boulangerie* will be closed, the owner having died from some mysterious illness which left him incapable of passing on the secret of his recipe.

So the Yorkshire Dales valley was nothing like the one in France but it reminded us of it because we stopped to drink tea and because of the feeling of exhilaration that comes from being high up, and the floaty hovering feeling you get from looking down into valley folds and vegetation and the crusty covering of frozen snow.

Up the A19 to Thirsk. As we approach a roundabout I'm studying the map, searching for the road we need to take and I look up when *le roi* says – it's OK, I've got it – meaning the right road. Obviously he had, because we went twice round the roundabout, found ourselves on Rhymer Street with Piper Lane leading off from it and had to turn back to find the right road.

Birds flying up like flecks of black, burned paper from a sooty chimney. A fallen tree in a field looking like a grave, reclining seal. We go to visit the Buddha, in the campus of York University. The first time I saw him was in summer, glimpsed out of the corner of my eye, half hidden by leafy trees. Hardly could believe my eyes or my luck at finding him. I'd no idea he was there, no-one at the conference I was attending had mentioned him. Larger than life-size, sitting cross-legged on a plinth-cushion. Pale green, sea-green. This time, because the trees are bare, he is much more visible than that first time, in summer. Sunlight falls on him. In his stillness, he seems to move, there is fluidity, mobility in his face and his magnificent repose.

In Northallerton after waking to fractured reflections, we have breakfast in Funk and Wagnell's Continental Café. We drive past more reflections, in a triptych window. Red roof-tiles and red brickwork lean across the mirror-vision, not matching up, like jigsaw pieces that just will not fit, no matter how hard you press together their resisting edges.

Was there a Mrs Buddha? asks *le roi*.

Not that I remember, I say.

Poor fellow. What he missed.

And I take his cool, so cool green hand in mine and press it silently, reassuringly, and think about the feelings that a lump of metal, a carved and wondrous image, an icon, an idea, a play of light, can arouse.

Depending on the words we use, it sounds absurd, it sounds most natural, most perfect. All of which of course, is unimportant. What matters is the feeling. Which is there. It's just the mind likes to play with these conceptions, toss them around, shrink them, amplify them, stretch them so the whole world is contained, reflected in it, like a tremulously thin-skinned bubble.

Here Buddha, here is my hand, slipped in your cool-smooth light green one, green as the inside of a cucumber.

3

Plank Music and the Berets of Bilbao

Waking in the early morning dark, and by the time we left the sky was all pale green, melon green. Ice on the windscreen, crispy snow on the pathway. On the drive to the airport the sky grew bright and dazzling.

Aytor meets us at Bilbao airport and drives us to our hotel, where Isaac Guillory is already installed. In the afternoon I go out on my own and walk around in the streets. In the supermarket I buy apricot and grape juice, oranges and chocolate. The sun bursts on the pavement, spilt from the hot sack of sky. I run into Isaac and we sit for a while on a small grassy roundabout, the sun on our arms and faces. We talk about the times long ago when the celestial world was never separated from religious beliefs and practices; days of omens, of 'a star in the east', days when people heeded their dreams and acted on them. He tells me that in Bethlehem, on the site where the Christ is supposed to have been born, there is a zodiac on the floor.

In the hotel room, the net curtains shiver, behind the opened window. Then the curtains fan out and the shutter, half-closed, rattles slightly. This is a place of warm winds, but many people, mainly older men, still wear black berets.

Aytor says the military wear red and the police wear white, but other people usually wear black.

The following day John and I go out together, exploring the city. We walk along narrow streets, following some unusual sounds. The street opens up into a square outside an old church where two young men are banging three planks of wood with two thick sticks of cylindrical wood. The planks are laid across a trestle and are of different lengths and so give out different tones. When we go inside the church, where the priest is intoning, you can still hear the wooden sounds outside, plank music. Groups of people wearing black velvet clothes and large black shady hats, wander through the old town, playing guitars and mandolins. In one of the squares, three men are playing, two with drums, one with a whistle with three holes, a kind of flageolet, with a

ring at the bottom, where you put your little finger. All the men wear black berets, in the Bilbao style.

There is a philosophy and a tradition to the wearing of the beret, as we discover when we go to buy one. They are worn in a certain way, perched on the top of the head in Bilbao, but worn further back, in San Sebastien. And in France they're worn at an angle. Black in Bilbao, dark blue in San Sebastien. They must always be worn with the same bit to the back *por conserver la forma*. And if they get wet, they must not be folded. They should be shaken, then laid flat to dry. Only when dry, should they then be folded. So that beret-wearing becomes a statement of identity, can be read, like a palm. Colour, angle and shape.

John insists I buy chocolate studded with nuts, at the *patisserie*. The nuts are curved like peeled bark from a tree. The assistant breaks it with a small hammer. We then buy a green paraffin lamp and watch the olive green river flow under the bridge. We hire a green car. We watch the pale green waves slipslide up the yellow-sand shore at San Sebastien.

At the meal after the gig last night, I tried a piece of John's squid. It tasted good, a bit like spongy chicken. But it distressed me that they are cooked in their own ink. Like an indignity.

*

In the green hired car we drive west along the coast road to Santander, heading for the mountains. Go-away clouds on the mountain-tops. Sea-waves with long white lacy shawls trailing down their backs. Forests of eucalyptus trees.

It began when we were driving through the mountains. The thin road wound up and down with such steep drops that I felt quite dizzy if I looked down. As it began to get dark there was an increasing sense of loss, of nowhereness, night pressing in, no space, no wide wings, no imagination, shrinkage, burial, immolation inside the skin.

Then the nightmares. I had to leave and I had nowhere to go. No plan, no direction, no money, no companion. I briefly wondered why I hadn't done something about this before. But too late now. Just a yapping little dog for company. And multiple variants on the same theme. I'd lost everything. Panic in the bones, dull, thick, powerful.

Roadside café
at the end of the line.
Everything passes,
all of the time.
Fugitive dreams
in trucks and cars,
hard metal shoulders
thick rubber tyres.

Dead end café
at the end of the line.
Everything passes you
all of the time.
Hell's stopover
at the side of the road.
Stay here much longer
and you're gone for good.

Empty your dreams
in the roadside bin
you won't need them here
in the truck-stop café
at the end of the line
in the truck-stop café
at the end of time.

4

The Juggler in the Night Garden

London. This morning was sunlight on red bricks, a narrow slip of a yard outside, sunlight skidding as if it's lost its footing, twirling in the gap between the buildings. I catch it when I look out of the kitchen window across to the buildings on the other side, other people's homes and kitchens, and I hold it in my hands, this light. This holding morning moment, in the little room next to the kitchen, with the white table, looking out into the yard, a gap between red bricks where sunlight can fall through.

James has made tea in a large brown pot and he sets it on the half-moon table that looks out onto the space between the buildings. In this small room, there are chairs around the table, a fireplace on the opposite wall, an entrance to the kitchen and the hall. So it is a station as well as a room, a place of passage as well as somewhere to be in, to sit round the table, to look out across the sun space to the red brick beyond.

The sun shows up the grime on the windows, the white paintwork peeling on the window frame outside and inside, the hall is half-papered, some strips torn off and a worn carpet underfoot, and my boots make heavy thudding noises on the floor and I like this flat, with its tousled appearance, like someone just waking up, or wandering into a morning kitchen, light falling on their hair and disappearing, as they move into shadow, light falling in jumbled patterns.

There is space in this flat, there are large empty spaces, they are gentle, they are hesitant, they are full of sun colours, they are sometimes lonely, but they have a taste of wings folded, a slightly musty smell, there is a sleeping love in this flat and I feel the light just stretching to wake it up, and I want to wake it and I want to touch it, I want to warm it with my fingers, I want to say 'wake up love', this is homecoming time, too much exile gathers dust on your hair and on your table, too much dust on your books and in your dreams, wake up and come home. Remember who you really are. The sun cups shadows, cradles them, tosses them carelessly across the little room, half moon room with two entrances, to let the light in and the light out.

*

The scene this morning is the harbour of a seaside town in south west England. In the backdrop (visible to the audience, as props to the imagination) are years of travel – ferries, trains, airports, check-in lines, stickers on guitar cases, battered travel-bags, guitars, accompanying players, blues in different countries; as Jackson C. Frank put it, 'The Blues Run the Game', only sung with slightly different accents, and more scene changes – mountains in Spain, *gelati* and gesticulation in Italy, sprawling billboards in America.

Here, the seagulls are cawing their way in and out of the harbour. Boat trips to 'Olde Worlde fishing port' of Brixham are advertised.

It occurs to me that not everyone sees life as an ongoing

quest for meaning and homecoming. I know very well where home is. I mean – when I am there, I know it. It comes and goes, like focus. Sometimes you just have to wait – like looking at 3-D pictures – where's the art and what's the trick and how do you tell others how to do it?

Oh, when I talk of love, some snarl, some scoff, some move away from me as if I've said something to repel them, hurt them, as if I am malodorous. Naïveté they say, turn it around and then it is my fault yes, I am at fault, I must learn other ways and lose the liquidness of it, the looseness, oh far too loose, naïveté. This slow and undefined, unborderedness – it's got to go.

They move away. So long. I'm leaving coast behind, slipping, spinning, circling down to the drowned cities of the mind. All the graceful statues are covered by the water (so I dreamed). Beneath the surface, the beauty of these wonderful creations is unseen. No-one knows they're there. Swimming underwater, in the harbour, I discover them. They are real and they are there.

Beside the harbour, where the tide is out, boats tilt into silt, that mud-sand mixture at the edge of harbours.

Love is what we're made of, love is what we are.

I feel these are quotations, and I don't know who I'm quoting. It's just this voice that breaks in now and again, with a quiet and insistent certainty that does not appear to have anything at all to do with the people who are moving in and out of gift shops, buying brightly coloured spades and buckets, beach balls, postcards and souvenir mugs of Torquay. Cafés called *The Tudor Rose* the *Rose Marie Fish Café* and *The Water's Edge*. What all this has to do with the Buddha's brimming gift of grace or the inner kingdom, or the garden, or this voice that slips through sometimes, in between a clanking noise somewhere just offshore, the harbour traffic and the nagging seagulls – I do not know.

How the inner kingdom links with Scottish bank notes unacceptable in a London shop, motorway maps we keep having to buy because they get torn and horribly abused, defaced, ripped and ultimately lost – well, this is part of the puzzle, a part I think I have to figure out. And sometimes I get glimpses, real clues, yes, like the other morning in a flat in Balham, with a threadbare carpet, peeling paintwork and one of those still moments, full of sunlight and the rustling of wings – a Presence, I might call it, so that everything is changed to gold.

Abingdon, Oxford

In the evening we travelled back across the country from Torquay to Banbury. Something happened to the light, it turned soft and the colours in the sky were an array of tones of pink and orange and red and purple and the lemon light and the crimson evening colours were all trying to pull us in, but we had to make it back across the country, we were late, and so we crossed a magic place and could not stop.

For the next part of our journey it was necessary to visit the Gate Keeper, he who controls the passage of the water and the ones who journey on it.

To reach his house you cross a tiny bridge with the water pushing through a narrow passage underneath you. The water stumbles with a muted roar between the walls of the canal. Colin is the lock-keeper and his house is right next to the canal. He operates the locks, controls the water levels and the passage of boats and he counts the people who fall in. And he rescues them if necessary.

After consuming quantities of soup and French *vin rouge*, we try some of Colin's home-made wine. It draws your mouth in, sweet as lemons, makes you gasp for more. Colin keeps these bottles on a high shelf which makes them difficult to reach. He stands on a chair and I hover round him, worried that he might not make it, might not be able to reach that high, or might lose his precarious balance. But he manages, we sit down again and gasp our way through yet another bottle of the shiny yellowsun wine. We praise it highly.

Is it all right? says Colin, swaying slightly in his chair.

Wonderful, we murmur, let's have more.

It's very late by the time we all, leaden-limbed, climb the slow steep stairs to the bedrooms on the upper level.

The next day we head for Sheffield. It is the first real day of spring. The magic place we touched the evening before, reappears, we enter it again in the morning, and it is like passing through a veil into a warm summer world, a still place where the light joins everything.

The venue for the Sheffield concert is the Merlin Theatre which is in a large house in extensive grounds. We meet Little Jack, the tight-wire walker, and I decide to have a go at wire-walking. Little Jack shows me what to do.

Look at the end of the rope – put your foot out, feel how you can balance yourself. Meet this stick. You're going to be good friends with this stick.

Thick wire between my toes, holding Little Jack's hand on the one side and the trusty stick on the other.

In the evening I sit out in the garden. There is a silver edge of Moon, a curved blade, sharp as salt sting, this bright sky-hook of Moon, this sickle hunger, drifting to a slow consummation with a dark blurred outline of a tree. I'm sitting in the magic garden, yew tree in front of me and the Moon blade about to cut the pine tree with its silver wing. This garden whispers a shelter place, all cupped with a dark sky and a tree curving over buildings, a pine protection.

Stars above the yew tree, and I am filled with this night, leaf shadows falling across the page, shadows from a light outside the broad and leaning house.

This is a sanctuary far from noisy traffic, packed bars and crowded cities. It is a total wonder. Rustling just behind my head. Little Jack is practising on the grass, rolling a transparent ball along one arm then onto another. I am hidden in this little alcove, this wooden bench set back from the yew tree.

Juggler in the night garden. The trees are full of whispering tonight, full of language. The light clacking of the juggling balls. The Moon has cut its way into the sky behind the tree. The tree has a light fire burning in its heart.

Little Jack picks up his juggling balls, dons his top hat, goes back into the theatre. Long poles of trees and a slight splash in the pond, a few feet below the wall.

The Moon comes out from the other side of the tree, a shining horn, a sharp, curved nail. A tree hook to pull the night down, hold it down, fasten it, secure it, throw your arms round it and hold it close.

I keep coming back to the garden in the darkness, its silence free of raised human voices, free of traffic sounds – but full of life, full of whispering trees, fishes moving in water, nesting barn owls, squirrels, a fox, a hedgehog. And the juggler in the Moonlight, in the night garden, just the soft clacking of the wooden balls.

.

5

Giardini Di Rocca and Good Friday in Leffe

After the Weavers gig in London last night we went to an Indian restaurant accompanied by Dave never-lost-for-words and his side-kick friend who elaborates, as a good chorus should, from time to time. Nick and James came with us as well as various other musicians. One of them was the pipes player who was called Paul, an Irishman, rather shy and quiet. I felt an immediate sympathy for him. You don't meet many shy musicians – mostly they're full of braggadocio, quick talking, part-time theatre managers, hiding vulnerabilities under the skin. In that respect, Paul hid nothing, so I felt I could relate to him right away. I could see he didn't like the bright stage lights. When he played he kept his talking to the minimum, when he messed up a note I could see the aggravation on his face. I hope he plays and plays forever, never stops, never gives in or gives up.

Some people seem to merge in with the stage lights, open their pores to them, or meet them in some place before they reach the skin, making a kind of magnetic fusion. Or perhaps they've just developed light-armour better, got more adept at it, through practice.

We stayed the night at James' flat and slept in, drove to

Heathrow, and just made the flight to Bergamo. Gigi, whose real name is Luigi, met us at the airport and he is driving us south.

The roads are lined with blossoming trees – apple, pear, cherry. The stretched vines are covered with buttons of white blossom, all round and full like burst seeds of light, all shining and hanging there, with the multiple vine arms all thrown open to the sky, chalice arms in their rows of light.

We are on the long road sweeping across Italy, distant mountains to the right, flatlands to the left. On the right are blooming trees, all white and pale green, and the gentle cypresses are dark, pointing up to sky. Sombrero spruces fan out into protective berets. The poplars head heavenward like the cypresses, all thin and light-flickering and there's the plane trees with saffron leaves and the vineyards with their black arms twisting in all directions. Rough dances, the notes of the vineyards writhe and quiver on a mottled page.

We see the first olive trees. Then more spear-tipped cypresses. The rippling of the language on the tongue, behind the cheekbones, in the throat. So thin and sweet and flowing, these unbroken words slip into the bloodstream. *Gelati parole*. Ice-cream words. All cool and sweet and trickling.

*

At Senegalia we have a meal of spaghetti and *fruto del mare*, salad and other wondrous concoctions with cheese, spinach, potato. Afterwards we walk along the beach, *mare verde*, finding shells with crazy zigzag patterns, and a starfish, a great treasure, *stella marina*. *El Maestro* found delicate round shells, paper thin sea urchins. The next concert is at Cesena and I decide to go exploring on my own. The gardens around the *Rocca Malatestiana* draw me at dusk. This red sky and the dark green trees, some rising straight up and some drooping, as if asserting their collaboration with the earth. The spruces spread their wide green fingers, guarding deserted paths up to this *Rocca*. There's no-one else around, just a cat slipping into the bushes. I get the feeling I should leave this until tomorrow and so I head back to the entrance gates. But when I reach them I discover they are closed and locked. They are very tall, these gates, and I don't think I can climb them. I go up the steps and look down at the sheer wall. It's quite a long drop to the pavement. I could do it, but I'd rather not.

I go back to the gates. When I see three girls walking past I call out to them, to attract their attention. They say they will phone the police and when they come back they explain that I will have to wait, maybe half an hour. But just five minutes later a police car arrives, with two policewomen. They tell me that there is an *otro ingresso*, if I just walk further up the path – and they will drive round to the other entrance. So I walk along the worn footpath that winds between dark and shadowy bushes, and I arrive at a gate with a hole in it, just big enough for me to crawl through. I then climb down the slope to the road, where the police car has arrived, blue lights flashing, just to make sure I'm at the right place. I thank them profusely and wave as they drive off.

I walk around the cobbled streets of Cesena, thinking I might have a cappuccino, to celebrate my escape from the locked garden. But I don't see any café and by now I'm tired so I head back to the *albergo* where we are staying. There is no-one else walking on the street apart from a young guy who attaches himself to me. I don't respond to his attempts to make conversation but he trails on, limpet-like, a soft sea-creature, and when he passes underneath a street-light I see that he is very young. I go into the *albergo*, pick up the key and climb two flights of stairs. The window of the room looks out onto the street and I see him still standing outside the door of the *albergo*, watching me.

I close the shutters, have a shower. When I go to bed, lots of shells and starfish dance in front of my eyes and I hear the sound of the sea in the background.

*

Perugia has terraces of red roofs, all sloping and slanting and tumbling downwards, all angles and sudden endings.

This town is the most amazing, the ur-city of Italian ancient buildings. It tops the lot. Its tiny narrow streets, its archways, shutters and peeling walls. Its huge church built like a fortress. The church bell sounds distinctly off-colour, slightly to one side of the note. Off-key, off-colour. It jars the ears a little, this discrepancy between what they would like to hear and what they're hearing.

The building where the concert is taking place has painted walls, arches and ceilings. Behind the stage, where John is playing, various coats of arms are painted. Above the armoured heads spring a variety of animals – lions, horses, dragons, crows. Some have trees with curved branches that form *vesica pisces* – weeping willow trees with an almond-shaped heart.

After the concert we're joined in the restaurant by a crowd of people – the promoters, some of their friends and a couple of John's friends from Rome, Paolo and Stefano.

Near Firenze, *Il Legenda* says 'Know thy Roots' in some similar way to the Greeks 'Know Thyself'. Mostly, our philosophical discussions only happen when he's drunk and as a result, he doesn't listen to me as I try to make pretty, precise, prinked-out distinctions, with the neatness of embroidery, mandala-mind, yes, in philosophical mode I want mandala-mind and *Il Legenda* is in swim mode, swimming like a slow docile fish through the watery associations of his ideas. Leading back to the one *integrale* manifesto, 'Know Thy Roots'. I translated it badly at first, as 'stick to thy roots' but was told this was not correct, one was allowed to wander apparently, once one was familiar with them, using them as strength, as sustenance, burgeoning through all new explorations and discoveries, enlivening them, as one embodies just the topmost, just the newest, the tiniest, most insignificant of leaves.

Olive trees on our right and only a few kilometres from Firenze. Olive trees also on our left. Terraced hills and cypresses in front. The beret trees, the spruces, all spreading and protective and the hat-pin cypresses, all trim and one-pointed, heading for the sky.

We see the roof of the Duomo as we pass, on the motorway. I point it out to *Il Legenda*, who peers through his specs and finally identifies it.

Oh yes, it looks like one of those sea-urchin things, he says, poetically.

Good Friday procession, Leffe

Santa Maria
Madre de deo
Prego per noi peccatori
Adess e a l'ora nostra muerte

The procession moves out of the Church, very slowly. The big cross is flanked by two people, bearing lanterns on poles. The priest's voice comes through the loudspeakers.

Ave Maria…

Next come small children, some of them with wings attached to their backs. Along the narrow streets there are flickering lights, high up on the walls.

Santa Maria…

Men wearing white lacy smocks are holding huge creamy coloured candles. The old ladies who are not married are dressed in black, with white lace covering their heads and shoulders.

Madre de deo…

Finally, the band joins the people following the first cross and eases into a mournful tune, only not quite a tune, but rather some slow, sonorous notes strung together.

Prego per noi peccatori…

The huge bier floats out of the church, borne on the shoulders of a dozen men, barefoot and dressed in white cotton shifts.

Adess e a l'ora nostra muerte…

And the men shuffle under the weight of the bier, which carries a prone plaster figure on it, representing Jesus. I get to thinking about ceremony and ritual and how, by imitating, by putting on the right, the appropriate costume, by making certain gestures such as walking barefoot down a cobbled street – and it is cold up in these mountains, there is fresh snow higher up on the slopes – carrying a heavy bier on your shoulders and trying to keep in step with everyone else, well – through imitating, you become the thing you represent. This is magic – not in the sense of something weird and wondrous though it does taste slightly of miracle in this sharp mountain air – but just simply, the way it works.

Prego per noi peccatori.

*

À la Eliot:–

> *In Cesena shadows followed me*
> *through cobbled streets*
> *and in Perugia I drew*
> *back the shutters*
> *and wrote postcards,*
> *late into the night.*

Leaving Leffe

Goodbye mountains, with buildings on top, without buildings; mountains with jaggy edges, like a lying-down face in profile. Yesterday, with their light brush of snow they looked polished, as if God had been out in the night, doing His housework.

Today, it is Giovanni who is driving us to the airport. He is large, solid and taciturn. He sits heavily as we drink our morning cappuccino, the sunlight falling in the window. But he is tired, they did not get back till 2 a.m. last night and it is not yet 9 o'clock in the morning.

Luigi had told us about statues of the virgin which have recently been weeping blood. First one, now several through-out Italy have been found to be doing this. Apparently it is not a hoax. When we pass a sculptor's yard, full of white plaster figurines I'm reminded of this. I ask Giovanni if he has heard of these weeping *madonnas* and he says that this is nothing new, stories of statues of the virgin weeping blood, and sometimes milk, have been told for as long as he can remember, it's part of the culture. But these stories intrigue me and I wonder what the Church will say to them. Will it dare to say – we do not know what's going on? We have no answers, it is real, but what it means, we cannot say? Or will it simply ignore the phenomenon?

Isn't there something in people that makes them always dissatisfied with what they have, where they are, what they're doing? What is this in people? I imagine there's a part of everyone's life which, if you scratch it, you'll find there's something they're not happy with, something they want to change for the better. Something that rubs, that irritates, that does not fit. Some badly fitting part of the costume, that needs alteration. Because it irritates, it gets attention oh yes, it becomes the pearl…

There's a part of Italy in the north where they would rather be German than Italian and if you speak to them in Italian (says Luigi) they answer in German. How strange, we think. It turns out this area used to be German but is now Italian. Imagine! Having been German and then being forced to be Italian!

Interview on the plane with *Il Legenda*:–

Q What is your favourite myth?
A I only have one. The mist that transcends all other mists. [He is sitting by the window and we are flying over France but there is so much cloud you cannot see anything and I think this influenced his answer. I change the subject and

say I want to use my new pen, just purchased in Italy, but not on a hangman, on something worthwhile and he calls me an insufferable snob. Snuffling, I sob into my British Airways napkin, it was never meant to be like this and when I was little I had coloured pens – yellow, green, scarlet and purple – oh, the purple biros, where are they now?]

Q What were your earliest influences?

A Peter Pan. This is how I learned to fly under windows so successfully.

Q Did you ever come across purple biros when you were young?

A Afraid I lived in era before invention of biros. Only pointed sticks for sand scratching, later the indelible pencil [i.e. no].

Drawing by John Renbourn

6

Hair Colour Mishap

I woke up in the night to the sound of rain against the windows. Then one flash of lightning followed by one peal of thunder. Drumming rain in the half light with some gravelly, sleepy, waking up dawn peering through the slats in the bamboo shutters. Six a.m. and some early morning traffic, full of promise and excitement, packed full, wisps of journey all lingering in the morning mind, all spacey and hovering, large and loose and streaming.

Today we're off to America. The flights are booked. Just before we left home, I decided to henna my hair. I got carried away with enthusiasm and decided to henna John's as well. But the results were not quite what I expected. Because John's hair is white at the sides the henna treatment turned it bright orange.

We drove overnight to London. Somewhere on the motorway we stopped for coffee in a steely kind of dawn. We were treated to breakfast at Nick and Judy's, then we caught the tube up to the embassy, to try to get John's visa. No, the doorman said, too late, the visa department shuts at 11.30. Come back tomorrow.

We walk along Oxford Street, busy, bright, full of bustling people. Two kilted musicians play funky bagpipes. We
pass an Indian shop in Soho, where I decide to buy more
henna, darker this time, with the idea – the hope – that the
application of dark brown henna might reduce the flaming
orangeness of John's hair. He has taken to wearing a hat.

In the evening we have a meal – a banquet – at Nick and
Judy's – couscous, chicken, a tureen of vegetables, strawber-
ries and cream and masses of wine. We get back to James'
flat about 2 a.m. and fall into a heavy sleep. John gets up
early to go back to the Embassy and wait in the long queue
for a visa. I stay in bed, to catch up on sleep. James has gone
out but he phones about midday to say that the key was
on the mantelpiece if I want to go out. About an hour later
there's a knock on the door. John is back, exhausted from
the early start, the general lack of sleep, from waiting for
hours at the embassy to acquire a work visa for the USA.
He's also badly needing a pee. I go to get the key from the
mantelpiece. I try to open the door but the key will not turn.

Why aren't you opening the door? John shouts.

James said the key was on the mantelpiece but it's not the
right one, it won't work.

Expletives come from the other side of the locked door.
As they seem to be directed at me, I shout my annoyance
through the letterbox.

I'm doing everything I can, how dare you shout at me.

Are you angry with me? he yells, above the traffic noise.

You called me a dikko, I heard you.

I was joking.

But I am hopping mad, blazing, and go searching
desperately for the key.

Will I phone James, at Nick's? I shout.

Well, if you feel like it, John shouts back. I phone. James

says to search under all the papers on the mantelpiece, but he'll be back in five minutes. I go back to report to the fizzling, exhausted, stressed-out, needing-a-pee orange-headed orangutan at the front door, but he's disappeared. Or at least, I cannot see him through the small rectangle of visibility afforded by the letterbox. I go upstairs, open the living-room window, lean out. And I see him outside, near the front door, writing a postcard.

I'm writing you a postcard, he says.

Well, I hope it's something nice I say, and giggle. He pushes it through the letterbox.

You are not a dikko, you are beautiful, he wrote on the postcard. And underneath – can I be in your pantomime?

As promised, James drives up in the car a couple of minutes later, and the door is successfully opened.

A brush with psychosis in Madison, Wisconsin

The skies have been clear all day, warm sun on our arms and faces as we walk across to the planes – from New York to Washington, then from Washington to Dayton, Ohio. But mostly it's been air-conditioned airports, aeroplanes, and hermetically sealed Holiday Inn hotels. Americans don't seem to like the effects of the elements. I'm used to wind, rain, cold, air at any rate, air, and this cushioned environment is a little strange.

Funny little planes from New York and Washington. They're like slightly dotty, wonky little birds, taking off easily, landing like a smooth dream, propellers whirring away. I watched a tiny little patch of light travelling over fields, turn into a black dot, then a minute shadow. As we came in to land the shadow got bigger and bigger, closer and closer and we met up with our own shadow when we touched down.

The flight attendant on the plane told us about the safety regulations as the plane was moving off but the noise of the engine was so loud that you basically couldn't hear a thing.

*

Waking up on the eleventh floor in the Days Inn, in the big room with big windows, sunny wide horizons, all big blue sky. John is still orange-haired, despite my efforts last night to henna it chestnut, it remains, utterly, determinedly, blatantly – bright orange. Although at the back it's now a lovely chestnut colour, the bits at the side are very bright. I'm used to it now, but when I first saw it I couldn't stop laughing; every time I looked at him, I just couldn't help it, though I tried to hold it in, contorting my face.

The Canal Street Tavern where John played last night, was a delicious mixture of old and new. There were stained glass panels on either side of what looked like an old fireplace and big wooden fans with brass fittings circulated slowly. The people were friendly and the atmosphere was relaxed. After the gig we went to Denny's to eat – omelette and chicken enchiladas with guacamole. Pierre Bensusan, a French musician, apparently had once been to Denny's to eat and declared 'this is not food' which I guess, according to French standards, is true.

Yesterday's flights were in tiny planes and when we bounced around for a while in the clouds it was like driving along a bumpy road. Today there are little puff pockets of cloud below us, like the tiniest and laziest of thoughts. Round and edged and perfect as little pastry circles, baby scones.

At moments like this, high above the earth and clouds,

things suddenly make sense. It's something to do with being in the moment, in the now, without all the worrying that clogs up the mind forming a big bottleneck, a long line. When things don't go smoothly there's a tail-back, and traffic jams in the mind.

Madison, Wisconsin has a good feel to it. Spring is late here too. We stay at the Edgewater Hotel, by the lakeside. Big bats and skimming ducks, board houses and swing seats in porches. Someone from the hotel is busy putting wooden jetties from the shore out into the lake. When I asked him why he was doing that he said that every winter the jetties were taken down, because the lake iced over. And only now, in late April, are they being put out again.

After John has left to go for the sound-check I walk the few blocks to the downtown area which has real shops. One sells an American version of Cornish pasties, another sells Indian and Peruvian things. There's a bookstore with life-size cardboard cut-outs of Jean-Luc and Warf, from Star Trek. I find a second-hand copy of Stevie Smith's *Novel on Yellow Paper* for only $5. Everyone is friendly except for an overweight teenager on a bicycle who approaches me as I come out of the pasty shop.

You should give yourself up, he says.

Excuse me? I say.

I saw what you took yesterday.

This is making no sense to me, and I simply stare at him.

I saw you shoplifting. You'd best give yourself up, the cops are on their way.

I head back towards the hotel. It's about a mile away and there are no other people in sight. He stays right beside me, cycling along the pavement. He monotonously repeats the phrase 'give yourself up', like an automaton. I try different approaches, explaining I could not have been shoplifting the day before as I had just arrived. Then I try to humour him, saying he'd been watching too much TV. At one point I get angry and tell him to go home, leave me alone. But he quietly persists with his tape of – give yourself up, I wouldn't like to see you spend months in jail. His persistence is menacing because he clearly inhabits a fantasy world and there is no shared area of communication. This, I thought, is what alien must truly feel like, no shared humanity, none at all. My legs feel weak and shaky as I walk along. I can't guess at his motives, though I try. Is it something about the way I look he doesn't like? Why? Is it obvious that I'm not from around here?

I look at his face, his eyes, trying to see beyond the mask. Is he trying to scare me because he intends to mug me or does he just enjoy doing this kind of thing? Does he do it regularly?

When I was in the pasty shop I asked the guy about the Club Wash, where John was playing. He said he knew it, he lived on that street, it was a good place and it wasn't far away. I had the idea to walk there because I'd not left my European way of thinking behind. I'm used to walking in any city I find myself in, I think of it as a basic human right. But the USA soon teaches you that it is not a right, but rather, a privilege. I remember now the pasty shop guy said something that I felt sounded a little odd, almost like a warning, like 'take it easy' or 'be careful'. I just remember it sounded off, discordant. It wasn't 'enjoy' or 'have a nice evening' and when I stepped out into the street this overweight teenager said 'you'd better watch out, the cops are after you.' I decided then not to risk going off into unknown areas and I headed back to the hotel, hoping he would eventually give up, lose interest. But he did not.

When I reached the hotel I went straight to reception and told the man there what had happened. He said he would do something about it and I went up to my room. A few minutes later the man from reception knocked on my door and assured me that the boy would not bother me again. He had gone outside and spoken to him and warned him he'd call the police if he kept hanging around.

*

The alarm went off at 5 o'clock this morning and it was barely light on the drive to the airport. Chicago airport again, with its dazzling, flashing strips of neon. The colours change all the time, they flash like short bursts of lightning, from one colour to the next. We're flying west to Orange County, California.

We've just passed the Grand Canyon, the ground below all purplish-red, orange and lizard green, river beds like snakes, curling, twisting, making all kinds of patterns, circular ones, curves and half-twists, gyrations of the earth, scattered with black poppy-seeds – spiralling poppy seed earth.

Layers and ledges of the Grand Canyon go up like steps, ridges, all red and brown stone steps. From here the river looks like a thin jewel, a turquoise string, a green snake. Reddish orange and grey-green are the desert's colours. Now it has turned to a variety of browns – from pale dusty desert brown, through greyish fawn to dark chocolate with a sprinkling of black pepper dusted on the brown mountains.

We're coming down now. These wavy lines in the ground are turning into mountains and the poppy seeds, into trees. Some low cloud is shaped into the mountains like a soft blanket, a white, downy shadow. Then suddenly we see the first buildings, arranged in large square formations.

The airport is called John Wayne. We are close to Los Angeles, but apparently this is a separate town. Lots of them are, though they all run together into one long urban sprawl. We are staying with Ken and Sharon and their house has its own garden, with orange and lemon trees and a fragrant creeper. We sit outside in the wonderful warm sunshine.

Sharon and Ken have two cats and two dogs. The dogs stay in one room and the yard, and the cats live in another room. They are obviously immensely fond of them, yet it seems an odd arrangement. The cats live in the room we're staying in, yet we heard nothing and only saw one of them, very briefly.

John's gig in the evening is in Laguna Church which has modern chunky stained glass windows. In the grounds there are spruces with big cones and soft green foliage that sprays out in clumps, like elegant dish-mops. There are also palm trees and another kind of tree with branches that start low and spread out wide. They look like the illustrations of baobabs, in *The Little Prince*.

Outside Laguna Church darkness falls among the baobabs and the tall eucalyptus trees with their long waving tufts of leaves, trees with long flowing dresses on, slinky tree dresses. John claims I stood on an ant when I stepped out of the car, but I don't think I did, or if I did, it was rubbery enough to bounce back.

I sit outside in the warm night with the cicadas singing and the sounds of guitar playing coming from inside the church.

*

The next day Ken drives us to McCabe's in Santa Monica, where John is playing his next gig. On the way we pass San Diego Freeway, Palo Verde Avenue, Redondo Beach, El Segundo, La Cienega, La Tijera Boulevard. There's a thin layer of cloud, but the sun is pleasantly hot and there's a cooling breeze. While John goes to check out a music shop Ken and I head for a diner. While we're waiting for John we talk about books and writers. He asks me – who are your influences? This seems to be a standard question and I don't have a stock response. The most truthful would be – the last writer I read and really liked. So right now it would be Stevie Smith.

Then there are Anaïs Nin, D.H. Lawrence, T.S. Eliot, Rosamond Lehmann. Maybe I could squeeze in Baudelaire and Verlaine, and Albert Camus for his spare, stark prose. Herman Hesse, for his deep, digging interest in the psyche, the soul, the nature of powerful emotions, their effects, their meaning and purpose in the scheme of things, the un-tearoutable spirituality at the heart of his writing, the powerful sense of quest – for meaning, identity, for some kind of order and the big place that emotional intensity has in our lives. He gives it room, he lets it in, gives it a central place, in a similar way to Lawrence. I think great writers have to be philosophers I mean real philosophers, explorers of life and psyche, explorers of the unknown. Because of what happens when you write. Because – sometimes – the act of writing can change you. It can create a process of transmutation, altering something from what it was, making it into something else. The alchemical process. I'm not saying that writing is the only way. But it is one way. Of peeling back layers, coming up with something new, so it becomes a process of discovery and of change, a process that sets free.

Neil Gunn, for the metaphysical ideas and atmosphere in his novels, the sense of quest, the way his writing leads you effortlessly into other worlds. David Lindsay for his vision, Knut Hamsun for the power of his description of inner states of consciousness.

Henry Miller's essays and later writing for its apparent simplicity, its directness and his exploration both of people and meaning. Dubravka Ugrešic for sweeping away all literary conventions and fixed ideas about what writing should be. Aleksander Hemon for his breathtaking writing, Rosalind Brackenbury for her descriptive powers of mood, feeling, place, Natalie Goldberg for her honed simplicity, honed to purity. Janet Frame's autobiographical writing for its visionary quality – like shivery images, you feel her perception is delicate and fragile and, like water, fluid, constantly changing, reflections on water.

And then there's Stevie Smith. With the lightness of her mind, shifting through a huge terrain of ideas, pictures, feelings – a tremendous honesty I feel from her writing. Non-judging. Simply – oh so simply (!) – depicting what is there, associations brimming over. Stevie Smith's writing is like jazz, elaborations, floatings off, from a theme. There's a sense of lightness and delight. She catches thoughts that often float away from us, just half-formed, like dream images and associations. As if she is dreaming at the same time as being awake.

7

The Forgotten Masterpiece in the Castle of Barge

We are in the dining-room of the *castello* in Barge, in the Piedmont area of northern Italy. There is a long wooden table in this room and I am sitting at one end and John is at the other. The sound of the river drifts in the open window and faint sounds of birds and the puffing and grunting of *Il Legenda* at work, composing (it is hard physical work this composing, arranging pencil dots with tails on narrow little lines, I can see how it could be hard to squeeze them into the little spaces and sometimes he makes a mistake and has to rub out one of the little round circles with tails, it has wiggled itself into the wrong position).

Well, in this very grand dining-room of the *castello* where we are staying, apart from the long table and the silky velvet-covered old chairs, there is a carved wooden dresser and other chairs, more ornate and less comfortable, with carved backs and those carved feet that I think are meant to resemble claws but look like four human toes, complete with toenails and the kind of ridges you get when you squash your toes against something.

There is also a picture on the opposite wall, a black and white painting showing a group of figures or rather, two separate groups. A young man sitting on the floor, at the foot of a lady's chair does not as I thought last night, have his arm draped in a familiar way over her lap, but his arm is bent and there is a bird, perhaps a falcon or some kind of hunting bird, on his wrist. He's wearing one of those soft floppy hats with a feather on it and a long, drapey kind of coat, with wide sleeves coming down to his elbow. He is gazing at the young lady with an expression resembling stupefaction, not so much a gaze of love or adoration but it's more of a can-I-really-believe-my-eyes kind of gaze, and he's rather pretty this youth, with fair hair curling gracefully down to his shoulders, but you get the feeling he's not enormously talented, but enjoys sitting at ladies' feet, gawping slightly, and he's forgotten to take off his hawk, which might be a little disconcerting for the ladies.

This is possibly why the one whose feet he is so daringly close to is not looking anywhere near him at all, it's as if he does not exist for her. The lolling young man sits on one side of her chair while on the other side, snuggling into the folds of her long dark dress, is a round drum, like a bodhran, only without the wooden crossbar.

So, this young lady is gazing out at you with a very satisfied expression, which might explain the young man's awestruck look. Her cheeks are round and plump as if she's storing two plums in them and her mouth is small and her whole expression verges on the smugly self-satisfied and when you look behind her to the second grouping you get an idea of why she looks so very pleased with herself.

Someone has just painted her portrait – she is in fact, the Mona Lisa, or a close relative of hers. The painter has just unveiled his work, to a mixed response. Leonardo – if indeed it is supposed to be he – is wearing a long tunic, partially covered by a wide-sleeved smock-like coat. It's obvious these are his working clothes, as compared with the finery of the foppish young man, the smug lady with the drum, her group of attendant ladies and a rather disdainful-looking lute-player behind her who has a severely crooked nose and a black beard and is concentrating grimly on his chords.

But to return to the painter – he is standing with one hand on his hip – the other rests on top of the ornate frame of his painting – but he still holds his palette and brush – this painting is obviously barely dry even though he's somehow managed to frame it without putting down his palette. A cloth is rolled back and rests on top of the easel, showing that the painting has only just this minute been revealed to the world at large. Though you could have guessed this anyway, from the fact that the model has not had time to change her position yet, apart from blowing out her cheeks to assume this smug expression, which is not shown in the painting and so must only recently have been adopted.

The painter is looking at two men, who are looking at the

newly unveiled picture. He is looking at them with an almost defiant, almost arrogant look, obviously someone proud of his work and aware of his own stature, daring them to be the slightest bit critical. Well, he needn't have worried about one of these onlookers. He's dressed in a similar fashion to weak-at-the-knees young Feather-Hat, who's still wearing his hawk, his joined palms are raised in front of his chest and he looks as if he's about to faint with rapture, that young man looks dizzy with the proximity of angelic presences, he looks close to being overtaken by vertigo, he's at the gates of heaven and if he doesn't stop gazing, he'll be in there, *tout de suite*, though it's unlikely anybody else will notice. The painter's too proud, Feather-Hat's too absorbed by the real thing, smug Miss Pea-cheeks who looks as though she's never held a drum in those limp fingers, never mind beaten one, is too involved with her own just-devoured-a-cream-cake satisfaction, her group of ladies are flicking the pages of a book and the lute-player is wrestling with his lute strings.

So the young man could rapturously collapse without so much as being an irritant to anyone, except perhaps the painter who might wish that he'd written a good review or passed on his name to a wealthy patron before zapping through the pearly gates at such unseemly speed.

But the other onlooker, now, he is in a very different position and you can see why Signore Painter has a wild-eyebrow'd look about him, why he's got all his defences lined up behind his teeth and ready to pour forth, for this other chappie is a tough customer and might even earn more credibility in some circles than the ready-to-collapse-in-rapture one.

This older man holds two books in his hand and by the simplicity of his flowing garb and the covering round his head, you could suspect some religious connexions, so the two books I'd hazard a guess, might be the Bible and a prayer book, so he's got his protection ready, if need be. And it looks as if he'll need it, by the violently contorted look on his face. This beauty is not saintly enough and besides, she's showing too much bosom and if this is meant to be the Madonna, this will not do, she looks much too sensuous, much too enjoying of the good things of life, she does not look at all like a virgin should look, she's got this come hither look in her eyes, no no this will not do at all, the man of the cloth is plainly about to burst with all these unexpressed feelings and he has even taken a step forward. Towards the painter? (perhaps to strike him down?). Towards the painting? (just to have a better look, to confirm his suspicions?). So that in the one instant, in the one place, both hell and heaven are about to be let loose and there's Miss Very-satisfied-with-her-portrait model in the foreground, her weak-kneed adorer, the ladies, and the grim-faced lute player, all innocently oblivious to what is about to happen.

La Donna (the painting) is about to be unleashed on the world and the lute player personally will not care because he's just broken a fingernail, the puffy-cheeked model will not care, because she never wanted to earn her living playing the drum and accompanying the grim-faced fella with the lute anyway and besides, Feather-Hat will clearly follow her anywhere she chooses to go and so she'll be able to dismiss those rather tiresome girls who spend their time reading books and missing out on a good time. And if that painting does become a best-seller, well, it will all be because of her, the inspiration. So really, it's just as much her work if not more so, than that painter guy, who's a bit eccentric anyway – personally, she's just glad it's over and done with. In a minute or two she might be able to move her cramped limbs – and doesn't anybody realise just what hard work it is, being an artist's model?

Ever tried sitting still for hours on end? And the worst of it is – you get foppish youths flopping down beside you, with a beady-eyed bird next to your elbow, and you can't move away. You're stuck with them. Still, he could be worse I suppose, he could be like that crazy painter who thinks the sun revolves around his ass, yes, he could be worse, that young man who has forgotten to take off his hawk, at least he'd never tell me to move a little this way, or to assume a languid and innocent expression which, believe me, is not easy to maintain for long stretches of time. No, he would never tell me what to do, look at him languishing, adoring, at my feet, a little simple he may be, but he is totally devoted and a supplicant so – he will do, but I must at some point, tell him to do something about that hawk.

*

Bells are breaking out all over the place. Chime after chime. There seems to be an awful lot of hours suddenly. It's not even 6 o'clock and I lost count well after six. In the corner of the courtyard there's a squarish, crumbling, red-brick tower. There are also columns skirting the paved area, the kind of columns that usually support something, like a grand and ornate entrance. Perhaps such an entrance was planned, but these stone columns do not support anything, although one of them has a greenish bust on the top, or rather, a head. It does not go with the grave stone column. It is leering in a slightly facetious, vacant kind of way, as if someone told a joke and everyone else laughed and he did not understand, but pretended to. It's that kind of a look – it would be simple if it did not have that slightly leering quality. But it could just be the tarnishing, the natural colouration, weathering, that makes it look, from here, somewhat less than angelic and more like a kind of wine-dulled satyr.

Barge is apparently famous for its stone, which it exports, even to the USA. This we discovered last night, when *Il Legenda* innocently asked if Barge was famous for anything, thinking historically, and Luigi said no and his friend said yes, for its stone, so this nearly started an argument. The stone is apparently cut into thin slabs, to make a kind of tile, and some of the rooftops here sport these diamond-shaped tiles, ranging from a light creamy colour to a shade of storm grey, the colour of the sky just now. On some of the old buildings the tiles have become weathered and rough and some of them have gone crooked and this looks very good indeed, these big skewed tiles, all rough-looking and irregular with suggestions of lichen and moss and other greenish growths in the cracks, these slidy roofs have a ramshackle, lived-in appearance, all age and history, an ageing squintness, a historical perspective, you might say.

So we have ended up in this rather tumbledown castle, with its dark wooden beams and its spiral staircase and its pleasantly faded grandeur. In the unoccupied rooms, huge tendrils of cobwebs are draped across corners of the ceilings. In the bedroom, just below the window, a huge fierce spider has taken up its abode and when I swept away a little of its web it waggled its legs at me most malevolently. Perhaps this was because it had just finished a massive meal of insect which I noticed squirming furiously at the web-corner yesterday. And which has now disappeared. The spider, truly, looks very big and fat now.

Yesterday we started off in Switzerland, narrowly avoiding being attacked – gunshot was heard nearby as we tranquilly made a cup of tea on the little cooking stove, outside the camper van. A loud noise in the distance. Coming closer. It sounded like an aeroplane using the road as a runway. It turned out to be an army tank. The quiet spot among the trees which had looked so peaceful and deserted underneath the stars the night before, was clearly being used as an army training ground. We decided to move on.

Movement in itself was not a problem, the difficulty was that, lacking a map, it was hard to proceed in the direction we wanted, since we did not know which way that was. In Interlaken *Il Legenda* was rudely spoken to, when he tried to change money. When he finally got some he bought milk and chocolate bars. But we were no closer to where we wanted to go, which was across the Alps, into Italy.

We were both fading fast, having had no breakfast and *Il Legenda* not even a cup of tea, because the milk was going off, though I drank mine all the same, tea with slightly off milk being better than tea without milk or no tea at all. Finally succeeding in buying maps, joy of joys, we found the road we wanted and headed for the mountains.

We discovered that to get through the mountains in-volved driving the van onto a railway wagon and being transported through a pitch-dark tunnel. The tunnel smelled of train fumes, like the underground, only much stronger. In the middle of deep mountain night, we casually told stories of rubble pouring into caves and tunnels, and mountainsides collapsing. Only when we emerged again, thankfully breath-ing in the fresh mountain air, did we admit to tunnel-terror.

After that, it was a long drive south and east, down the side of Lake Maggiore, with its seaside holiday-makers, that rather grim feeling of seaside or lakeside, and determination to enjoy and spend money and be on holiday, loitering, not knowing what to do. I imagined a story of crime, revenge, passion and desperation, taking place among the languid, slightly bored holidaymakers of the resort on the shores of the lake.

It got warmer, it got – almost hot, almost that baked summer feel which I crave, a longing to feel sweat running from the body, with a light wind to keep you cool. It did not last, for today is cloudy again, with a far-off heavy sky. Like God's dangling parasol, these motionless clouds are all bulgy with rain like a stored-up bad mood, all sulking, waiting to turn to rain, but not sure if they're going to, because that's just the way they are.

The bells start up again.

Señor Siesta lights up a fag, flicks pieces of rubbed-out pencil from his manuscript paper and mutters to me that I'm mad.

So we sit, one at each end of a long wooden table, silently scribbling, in a down-at-heel castle in Barge, Italy.

*

There was something quite distinctly magical about that castle. After a night when I simply could not sleep for no reason other than I felt wakeful, I got up and watched the sun come up, dark red against the greyish blue light of the sky, a soft sky and the soft colours of the pale blue and slightly yellowish rooftops. And the birds waking up and me sitting at the long wooden table with a soaked, unshiftable sense of peace. In the shivery light and the echo-y birdsong, I flitted from the bedroom to the kitchen and the dining-room with its long wooden table, and the room outside the bedroom with another long table and windows everywhere, looking onto the courtyard on one side and the rooftops

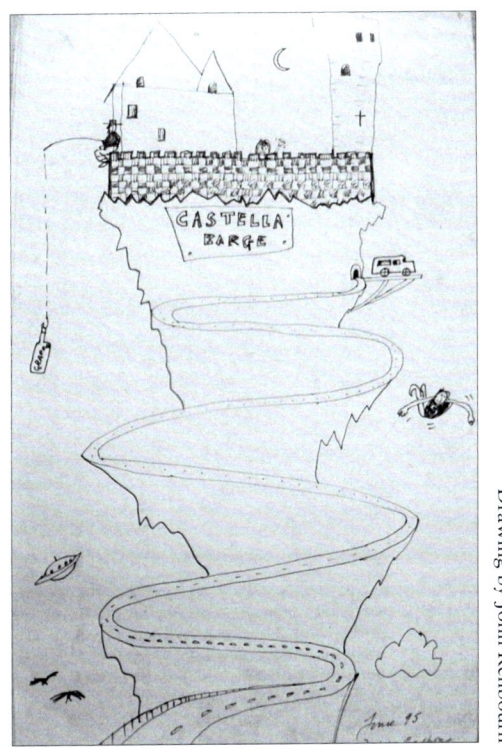

Drawing by John Renbourn

of the town on the other, drinking tea, in the damp warm dawn, all stillness and the birds.

Now for some reason I think of Colmar, where everything seemed to fall into place. The Grünewald paintings were easy to find, *Il Legenda* bought a pair of shoes that he liked and I found a book by Elsa Triolet, whose one novel I've read made me want to read more.

It was hot in Colmar. The heat had only just started to penetrate the clouds two days before, driving from Barge to Alessandria, via the coast. The whole coastline of north Italy is stitched with towns, or so it looks on the map, a hedgehog of a coastline, place names protruding into the sea like quills. We stopped at one before Genova, and found a rocky little patch of stones, boulders really, and after dipping tentatively in the water, we arranged ourselves on a boulder while the sun came out from behind a fleece of clouds.

The sun got into its stride when we left Alessandria the next day, after the last concert, an open-air performance in the Piazza del Liberta, with a sound system that made John compare the performance to a visit to the dentist. But they loved it he said, with a mixture of wonder and puzzlement.

The hotel room's balcony looked out onto other people's balconies and a big yard. This was very different from our castle at Barge. Getting out of the *castello* had been quite an operation. We had all our things packed and in the van, parked beside the trees in the courtyard. From here, the driveway led down to the road by the river, where you crossed the bridge to go back into the town. So we set off, but when we came to the huge wooden door at the end of the driveway, we discovered when we tried to open it that it was locked. The keys for this massive wooden door were lying on the table outside Luigi's room. When we came out of the castle, at the bottom of the spiral staircase, I had pulled the door to behind us. So we could not get back in.

But I'd noticed another stair going up the front of the building, above the part that was converted into a bar. There was a door at the top and when I climbed up, I found it was open. It led into a kind of lumber room, a store room filled with chairs, bits of tables, some old mattresses. One of the tables was on its side, with carved, lion-like protuberances emerging from where the legs joined the table top. I crept through this room then through the door at the far end, through a short passageway and then emerged in the long room next to the bedroom – then went on into the great dining-hall with the picture of La Donna, and the long table.

And there were the keys lying on top of the table. I picked them up, returned the way I'd come and went down to the massive wooden portal and opened it up. John drove the van through and I snuck back up the stairway through the lumber room and replaced the keys on the dining-room table. And so we left the castle in the early morning, without disturbing anyone.

8

Bardstown Festival, Kentucky

Pat Kirtley, musician, picks us up from Louisville (pronounced Loöville) airport. He describes a little music shop he discovered in Arkansas, that was owned, he said, by a 'hippy' (Pat is not a hippy) who had musical instruments from all over the world, including an oud from Egypt or Turkey. Pat plays oud music on a tape as we drive to Bardstown. The distinctive rhythms, he says, are made from playing scales.

It is hot. The sky has a pale, anaemic look to it, with the clouds only slightly lighter round the edges and in the middle, greyish-blue, almost the same shade as the sky. We began our journey with the overnight drive to Gatwick, then the eight hour flight to St Louis. We dozed off now and then. We flew in over the St Louis arch, then took the next flight to Louisville. Wonderful, to step out of the airport about 9 p.m. and the sky all red with the sun going down and the air warm and damp. Though I don't suppose the temperature, even now, is particularly high, the air is always warm and that's the difference between American heat and British. Even the nights are warm.

It sounds like a song –

Oh Babe, don't you know
when I'm with you
then even the coldest
nights are warm.

Except, unfortunately, it's trite and overused already.

This is bluegrass country. I suppose that name has the same origin as the Blue Ridge Mountains – the haze in the air turns the green grass blue –

Oh, the haze in the air
turns the mountains to blue.

Bardstown Folk Festival. Arlo Guthrie sits behind his big bus. The area where his bus is parked is taped off, presumably to prevent people straying in, though someone says the movie to be made should be called *Free Arlo Guthrie*. On the front of his bus, where the destination is usually shown, *Hanuman* is displayed.

The sun goes down among the trees, all red and twinkly, sparking in between the branches.

Pat is making a video of John. Pat's sister from Arizona is friendly and effusive and wants to come to Scotland. Everyone wants to come to Scotland. I try to tell them about the bad weather, but they complain about the weather here. It's so hot and humid in the summer, they say, with temperatures of 110 degrees – and then there's so much snow in the winter. I can only conclude that most people don't like the climate where they live.

The lightning bugs have started up and I tell Matt, our driver from the hotel to the Festival, how good they look.

You don't have them in Scotland? he asks incredulously. (He's only 19.)

Arlo Guthrie plays a few songs. He has long crinkly hair – a silvery white colour. He breaks off in the middle of some songs and starts to talk. Everyone loves it, of course.

Near the end little Matt disappears and comes back with a poncho to keep me warm, because he'd noticed I was cold.

John and Pat are on stage today along with two other musicians, called Ken and Dave. (All the soundmen and most of the people we meet, are called Ken or Dave, with the occasional Steve.) Someone sitting next to me in the audience says to her companion, it's interesting that he's kept his original hair colour at the sides, but he's going grey everywhere else.

She's talking about John. I consider leaning across and saying, actually, that 'original hair colour' (which is bright orange, not a natural shade of hair I have ever, anywhere, encountered on anyone's head) is henna-dyed but I decide not to spoil her illusion.

Ken describes himself as 'the thief of DADGAD'. (DADGAD is a special tuning invented I believe by Davy Graham and adopted since then by many guitarists.) Oh well, it gets some laughs. He plays slow, sensitive music. He's made two self-deprecating comments, saying he's not particularly talented etc. The people's personalities interest me just as much as the music they play.

Armadillo country, Austin, Texas

Instead of flying from Louisville to Chicago then to Austin as planned, we were rerouted via Dallas because of storms. On the way we passed through enormous clouds. John said that from the window seat, he could see lightning darting in and out of the massive banks of cloud.

It was 90 degrees when we arrived in Austin at 7.30 in the evening. The shoe-shine booth in the airport was closed. We hired a car and drove down Interstate 35, past the motels that line the side of the road, into the downtown area. John is looking for the Driskill hotel where he says he's stayed once before. We located the university where John will be playing, then continued downhill to the Colorado river. People are crowded onto the green area by the river, because it is the 4th of July and there will be a fireworks display.

Eventually we find the Driskill, which turns out to be a very grand affair. It is an old, a really old building, dating back to 1886 and nearly pulled down in 1969, so I read in the brochure, when the craze for erecting tall skinny buildings really took hold. People protested – concerned citizens got together and the building was saved. Strange, this American compulsion for demolition, when they're so desperate for history and anything old.

It's very plush and ornate and not one of these modern places that have all kinds of conveniences, yet lack something that you could call individuality. This place has plenty of it. It was built from a desire to make something beautiful, rather than purely functional. The foyer is enormous, high-ceilinged, wood-panelled. The receptionist wears a snoopy tie.

From the bedroom window we watch the fireworks going off, rising up from the river, clearing the skyscrapers and filling the night sky with brilliant patterns that fade so quickly, leaving dribbles of smoke. In the morning the sunlight falls like thin reeds across the tall buildings in the opposite street. But there are big clouds moving quickly across the sky. On the other side of the street there are white tables and chairs on the pavement next to some small trees. The awning has TexMex written across it, in huge letters.

I walk down Congress Avenue and stop at a deli which has tables outside, with awnings over them. This reminds me of Europe, these outside café tables with awnings, so I decide this is the place to sit down for a while. One of the differences between America and Europe is that in Europe, people like to sit outside cafés while in the USA, people like to sit inside, where there is air conditioning and so it's cooler. So these outside tables are quite a find.

Another difference between Europe and the USA is, of course, that people walk much more in Europe and there are far more people on the streets. So that sitting outside in America can be a bit disappointing as there are not a lot of people to watch. Anyway, here I am, sitting at a table on Congress Avenue and it is not too hot, the sky is overcast, there is a storm-feeling to the air, there is a breeze, the air is damp but a neon sign says it is 83 degrees. I have a regular coffee and a lemon-seed muffin.

Old wooden boxes on wheels, dark brown wood and dark green panels, coast by gently, more like boats than streetcars. They look very old, as if they have come out of a 1940s film-set and this is very comforting, like a memory of something so long ago you cannot really remember it at all, yet somehow it feels familiar and you cannot explain the familiarity of something that existed before you were born but there it is, old, comforting, reassuring, like the swaying boat buses along Congress Avenue.

The Driskill hotel too, gives me that feeling. It may not be the most stunning architectural feat ever conceived, but it does have a kind of vision, an old-fashioned grandeur, a sense of age and time that I feel hungry for, a sheltered, protected kind of feeling. So much in the USA is enormous and sprawls across the landscape – the huge billboards and neon signs – while the giant plaster figures of bulls and chickens outside restaurants leave you in no doubt that food is taken very seriously here and its preparation, cuisine and advertising creates a kind of folksy art form in itself.

Across the road is the Congress Avenue Card shop that sells souvenirs. On the front it has pictures of the State Capitol, the lone star flag, and an armadillo. There are posters for 'Moonlight Towers' – only found in Austin, Texas. The posters are attached to the street lamps and the 'towers' themselves look like elongated thin iron posts, with four 'lamps' at the top, casting a fuzzy light, like four white fluffy berets.

There's not much happening on the sidewalk. A girl walks past, with a green umbrella – not for rain. Street-sweepers come with long-handled dustpans and yellow brushes.

I walk back along 6th Street to the hotel and it begins to rain – fat drops descending unexpectedly from the sky and by the time we've checked out and loaded the bags into the car, the sky has cleared and the sun is out, and we walk along to the Old Pecan Street café and have lunch.

In Muhlenberg County
Wendell Cornet wore blue dungarees,
did not say much,
but pulled out chairs
for us to sit on
and played us tunes
on his banjo.

His music store seemed to me
in the middle of nowhere
though nowhere, in America,
is not a difficult-to-get-to place.
Spread out on the edges of small towns,
these places are nowhere
you could walk to.
But in cars they take no time at all to reach.
I rearrange my definitions of
'nowhere'.

TEXAS NIGHT

The shoe-shine booth is closed
in Austin airport.
No more shiny shoes today.
But I've got my K-Mart $14 dress,
my red straw hat,
I've got the hot wind from Mexico
and fat and sudden raindrops
from a passing storm,
a shaking, finger-picking
shoulder-licking storm.
And these hunched barge-clouds
go slouching by.

Wet fingertips
outside the old Pecan Street Café.
Box buses roll like boats
down Congress Avenue.
The storm wind shuffles
the bendy branches of
the sidewalk trees.
They float on windstream –
green and restless arrows,
tugging to be following the wind.

Oh, can't you just feel the
wet air on your face, when
the folk-singer plays
The Mist-Covered Mountains
on a hot and storm wrapped Texas night?
Can't you smell the stacked peat,
drying by the roadside?

Here, the green-panelled
wooden buses sway down
Guadeloupe Street. The awnings
flutter in the wind.
The air folds softly round you,
a warm, damp blanket,
sticking your clothes to your skin.
You walk slowly, slowly,
in this humid night.

Mist, mountains and peat-smoke
all seem far away
from the White Rabbit
and the Armadillo Restaurant
and all the colourful façades
of Sixth Street.
Outside the Cactus Café
the crickets blue their raspy music
through the night. Soft, splashy
sounds of fountain jets.
We listen to Merle Travis
and Kentucky Mountain Music
as we head north in Highway 35.
Dodge pick-ups, Fords and Cadillacs
hiss softly past,
on this hot and heavy Texas night.

Ann Arbor, Santa Barbara, Berkeley, California

Downtown Ann Arbor has a European feel to it, there's a sense of time here, a settled sense, of continuity and custom, of life being slightly weathered and worn, handled and enjoyed. After John's gig at The Ark, we eat pitta bread and French fries in the Fleetwood Diner, on the corner of Liberty and Main St. We sit outside. Someone comes by on a bicycle, putting up posters.

This day has been stretched, pulled at both ends, as we flew across the country from Detroit Michigan, and then had a two hour drive from LA to Santa Barbara along Ventura Freeway – El Camino Real. On the beach at Santa Barbara, walking in the sand to dip my feet in the Pacific, the ground beneath me started to shift and go uncertain. Vertigo shiver, from too much movement, this uncertain sand. And the foggy palms. Are we really here? John asks.

To reach where we are staying, we're told – Take 101 South, turn off at Casitas Pass, go right to Carpenteria Avenue, about half a mile further on turn left and you're there – Motel 6.

That lonesome train
from the cotton belt to Santa Fe
whistles a forlorn refrain
to the guitar music
from the open window
of The Underground
at Santa Barbara.

Isn't life strange,
with its heaven and hell embrace?
This duality, this yes/no,
this right/wrong, this
long-drawn-out affair with
judgement?

That lonesome freight train
whistling, hollering
and hooting through the night.

In the second half of the concert I dozed off in the car, heard the whistle of the train, a mournful hoot as it crossed the road half a block away.

After the gig at *The Underground*, Santa Barbara, John looked in at Matt's Grog and Groceries and made an amazing find. Three Castles tobacco is supposedly not made any more, in the UK anyway – but it was on sale here, so he bought several packets.

The next day is over the Bay Bridge, to Berkeley. A meal at the China Station, a restaurant which is a converted train station but freight trains still go past nearby – like the Southern Pacific – Cotton Belt, for Santa Fe.

Evening gig at the *Freight and Salvage*. Telegraph Avenue

at night – round midnight. Cody's bookshop is closed and even the Mediteraneum (sic) isn't serving coffee any more. A pair of boots lies on the sidewalk. The night is warm. We call in at a store for ginger beer and orange juice. Four hours later we're up again. Five a.m. and it's still dark, driving through the quiet streets, back over the Bay Bridge. This time we're on the top level and can see out across the bay, with the view of the lights of San Francisco, its tall building-block skyline, lit with pimply yellow lights.

*

This has been a varied and exotic summer. We have dipped in and out of seasons like a fruit machine, each state or county with its own angle on the weather, its own climate, its own variety of summer. Flying from Kentucky down to Texas, there were massive storm clouds in the sky, banked like the palaces of gods, vast structures that looked solid, light-infused with edges on them you could cut your fingers on. Shafts of lightning, flickering among these massive boats of cloud.

There was the gentle weather in Kentucky with everyone saying – isn't it cool? And the awning stretched between trees, for the audience to sit under, with mock-leaves tucked between its stitches, so that it was like sitting underneath a spreading tree, with little splashes of sunlight getting through.

There was the damp and heavy Texas heat and the hot sun as we drove along Ventura Highway. There were the misty palms in the cool evening on the pacific Coast at Santa Barbara. The light, delicious Boston sun, pale and crackly as paper, sitting in Lillian and Aaron's garden in the morning, in a Boston suburb. That was the beginning of our trip back home. Three flights later, we were back in London, in a muggy morning, with everyone exclaiming at the heat.

9

Dublin Trains and Perilous Coastal Waters

We are becoming such travellers, so good at shuffling in and out of seasons, that it's playing havoc with my driving. I have to think, before moving out into the road. It's no longer automatic, as to what side of the road I should drive on.

But as I prefer not to drive in cities anyway, I take the train or bus whenever possible and today it's the squealy train from Tara Street station, not the nimble, lightly sprung Dart train, with its green and yellow sides and its slanty lettering giving the impression of pure and unalloyed swiftness, one-pointedness and intent, wind in the hair and arrows flying through the air – no, today it's the lumbering, heavy-footed mainline train, that squeals its metal bulk to a slow, oh so slow, standstill, making people put their hands over their ears and cry out.

Not that I did either. I was secretly delighted to be boarding this ancient carriage, pinnacle of the pioneering adventurous spirit that created trains and railways in the first place – vehicles of adventure, lined with soft fabric like fake fur, with high-backed seats that made you feel you were alone, in the nice way of being alone, the pleasant way, the unintruded-upon way, that is essential for travelling within the privacy of your own make-believe world, populated by whatever friends, ghosts, demons and daring feats of adventure you care to think up.

In the modern trains, the fast dash, the light slipping of metal on the rails, there are no high-backed seats, the carriage is open and so your thoughts are too, or so it feels, and you have to guard them, or slip behind held-up newspapers and, in this hot weather, you stick uncomfortably to the plastic seats. You also hear other people's conversations which you do not want to hear.

But in these magnificent old trains, with their bulk, solidity, sense of grand purpose and unoiled brakes, you are still travelling in the grand style and I look out at the rooftops and through the gaps in the buildings and we stop at Pearse Station, with another stately entrance and loud announcement of our intention to stop and with an equally slow, regal, unhurried departure.

Through these gaps I see Kitty O'Shea's pub, just across the road from the recording studio, and a little further on, the Spar Store where I've shopped for French bread, cheese, orange juice and chocolate and slowly, oh so slowly, the great king of the train world pulls up at Landsdowne Road which is my stop and I get off, go through the subway to the other side and walk up the tree-lined avenue, pretending I am coming home from a busy day at work.

*

From the south coast of Ireland we take the boat to Bere Island. It takes all of five minutes. There's room on the little ferry for two cars, a few bicycles and foot passengers. The day before, arriving in Castletownbere, we saw the ferry, waiting to cross. It was raining. A solitary dun cow stood on the ferry, her head lowered, tail hanging straight down and the rain coming straight down on her too.

But this morning the sun is out and we go to look for the house John first saw two years ago and liked the look of. It is not easy to find. A gate that was once painted blue and the faintest suggestion of a path. Lots of butterflies – red, brown, orange and white. As we get closer to the house, a profusion of brambles and gorse bushes. Trees round it – apple trees, larches, fir trees. The area that was garden is now grass. Long, but discernibly garden. A view down onto the sea. The house, hiding behind the trees, almost shy. I unhook the wire holding the door closed and go inside. Wooden staircase, small rooms. It's damp, but could be cosy. A little house, abandoned, snug behind the trees, slowly being covered by brambles, it is very appealing and we both like it very much.

Then we decide to go down to the sea. Now, this is not a great distance. On a path or road it would take ten minutes at the most. But it's an area of bog, marsh grass and gorse bushes. Sometimes we are up to our thighs in this thick grass and gorse combination and sometimes the grass gives way and our feet squelch in the bog water. But finally we arrive at the thin line of rocks at the sea-edge. They are covered with seaweed. The parts that are not covered with seaweed are covered with barnacles. This is painful when you sit on them, your bare bum on the barnacles. I take my clothes off to try to make the slippery descent into the water. I do make it, almost to my armpits, but it's difficult to keep a grip on the barnacled rock and I'm not going to let go of it, for beyond that is a bank of seaweed and a blue line of rope connected to lobster pots, and I cannot just let go and launch myself into the water, partly because of the cold and partly because of the tangly seaweed, which I am sure will wrap itself round my ankles and drag me into the briny deep.

Well, once I've got back out, drying out, sitting on my T-shirt, John sees a Portuguese man o' war, a jellyfish-like thing made of a blubbery translucent, soggy-looking substance, fringed with black dots which move rhythmically. There it is, floating in the mess of seaweed, just beyond the small area of clear water that I'd half succeeded in lowering myself into.

Look at that, he says. If they sting you, you're a goner, an ex-person, this is when you go to meet your Maker, when the happy hunting grounds do call.

Well, he'd had too much sun and a staggering amount of exercise, pitching and ploughing through the swampland, gripped by the razor pincers of the gorse, but I thought he looked at my near-fatal encounter, my much too proximate demise, with too much equanimity, way too much calm.

(At the moment, he is making yet another attempt to read the Preface to the *Volume of Irish Fairytales*. The preface is written by W.B. Yeats. I have also tried to read it, with spectacular lack of success. After a couple of sentences, which are a bit like jazz improvisations trying to explain themselves in the language of Old Etruscan, the concentration wanders, words unstick themselves from the page and wander off, like seed-down from flowers. It is very hard indeed to keep these words on the page, harder than that even, to extract meaning from them, and hardest still, not to wonder, once you do get the hang of what he's trying to say, if the effort was worth it anyway. Great poets do not necessarily great preface writers make.)

Although I did not have an encounter with the vicious opaque blubber with the stringy trailing tendrils, I did get badly scratched by gorse and briar and far worse, bitten by anonymous bugs. I was wearing shorts and I now have huge red itchy blotches on my legs. Although this tends to happen to me every summer, these are particularly spiteful bugs.

10

The Railway Carriage Diner and the Boston Skyline

Driving in a bus from one part of JFK airport to another, there are planes landing almost every minute. A speck of light in the sky turns into a big silver rushing thing pouring itself towards land and then the puff of blue smoke as the wheels hit the hot tarmac, the welcoming earth. Queueing in a line to take off, there's an outsize plane in front of us, dwarfing our tiny propeller plane.

Nearing Boston there's a few clouds, flat-bottomed, rounded backs, outstretched wings, like planes. After landing we hire a car, drive out of Boston, following the Route 90 West, the Massachusetts Turnpike, with the symbol of Paul Revere's large-domed Quaker's hat. We turn off to Worcester, have a Mexican at the Acapulco Restaurant and find a room at the Worcester Motel, a run-down little place with a friendly manager.

John has a terrible coughing fit in the night. He feels he can't breathe and thinks it might be a reaction to what they use to fumigate the place against roaches. I'm so tired I'm only vaguely aware of what's going on and didn't realise till this morning that he stayed in the car for most of the night.

In the early morning sunlight I walk to a diner to get us some tea, to go. And so we drive along Route 9, but we soon stop in Fitchburg, enticed by a sign saying *Book Sale*. It turns out it's a sale of old library stock – $2.50 per bag of books. A bag holds about twelve books. We buy one each. We now have two heavy bags of books to take with us across the country, as well as everything else.

It's in the mid-80s when we arrive in Northampton.

*

The hotel restaurant at the Northampton Inn, where we are staying, is full of clinking and repressed silence, so we drive downtown to Kathy's diner, an old railway carriage, with an outside table where old men sit, one of them blind, one of them shaking and one called Pete, who is wearing a bright orange baseball cap. I'm outside having a cigarette, before breakfast.

You're rolling your own, remarks Pete to me. I nod and smile at him. Pete has a gentle face, a shy, shrugged way of sitting, slightly hunched, slightly turned away from me. Would you like a Chesterfield? I say no thank you. The young waiter with the ring of seeds round his neck looks out to say my breakfast is ready.

The blind man with a hoarse, reverberating voice, makes his way into the diner, uses the phone. His voice isn't just gravelly, it's echo-ey, electronic, it's a radio voice. He speaks to Helen, talks about a woman he's met, nothing sexual, he says. His voice has a very filling quality, it fills the whole diner and John thinks it is the radio, he says later.

At the end of the conversation he says I love you Helen and he repeats this and there is nothing sentimental or maudlin, perhaps his artificial vocal chords (for they must be) have this supreme advantage, that they cancel out traces of self-pity or attempts at manipulation. Like someone reading someone else's lines, they have the objectivity of distance and discretion, and you listen, because the emotion is even-tempered, not absent no, not absent, but not identified with, and therefore safe. There is nothing potentially wild or aggressive about the tone of this emotion.

En route Boston–San Francisco

Little streaks, flares of bright, fiery cloud skim past the plane's wing. Sometimes, they don't slide down its grey metal skin, they ignite it and it's a burst of light, wings on fire, just outside the thick-paned little window. That's all you can see, a chute of wing and a tiny area of blue beyond. We're above the clouds now, out of that shoal of light flares that the ragged bits of clouds became, as we moved up through the rain-making areas, the sky's swamp country, to where clouds were thin enough to mix with sunlight and combust into some inner sanctum of the light, light split open and revealed, trailing across an aircraft's wing.

Higher up now, much higher, only baby clouds here, nothing fearsome or scary, just little bumps and nodules on the sky skin. When we drove through Boston (the great, the glorious, the guardian of American heritage, allowing the old world flavour to flow under the tongue of the new one, tasting, testing) the familiar skyline spoke of history and sanctuary and imperturbable solidity. Fat as a bank and mortared with time, cleaned and clipped and satisfying, oh so satisfying, only the slightest trace of smugness round the trimmed parks and the brightly painted clapboard houses.

Boston can afford a little self-congratulation (nothing too exuberant or ostentatious mind you, subtle is the word, tasteful, like a thin kohl-ring around the eyes). I think I'd feel it too if I was it, entrenched, secure, serene and not a little pleasing to the eye, washed with its laps of time and loops of road and red red brick.

Some of the slim-line tower blocks grab at the passing clouds as if their great delight is to run their red-brick fingers through the steamy haze and turn the solid definition of a true blue cloud into a ragged tangle of stringy rain.

Tower blocks are like heads yearning for their cloud hats – or they could be. Though they look a little more like fingers trailed in water – a loving consummation of sky-messenger and tower block, sometimes caught, sometimes trailing, sometimes winged and always wet. Waving. Straight red bricky fingers are not drowning, definitely not, they're waving.

Wet morning this, beginning dull and overcast, first hour spent packing – not just clothes and bag and backpack, but the big box of books we'd acquired in Fitchburg library, when they had their sale. John had the brilliant idea of packing them up and posting them to us, rather than carrying them from one side of the USA to the other and then back, and then on across the Atlantic. A large cardboard box and parcel tape and 'tis done. Across from the Post Office, at Kinko's Copies, I get large adhesive labels and a marker pen and we're all set. The twenty or so books which cost us $5 to buy, cost $66 to mail home.

Then it was back to Kathy's diner for another mega-breakfast of eggs, flat sausages (that taste herby and delicious), fried potatoes and rye toast. Mr Radio Man with the resonant voice is talking to a woman sitting at the counter. Later he goes out, guided by his friend who'd been sitting outside the day before.

Someone in the booth behind us was talking about God.

My idea of God is – well, it's like nature I guess, it's natural, in nature, in life and the seasons, that kind of thing, he says.

It's only after we left the diner and joined Interstate Highway 90 East, that the rain really began. Big silver-grey puffs behind the cars and trucks.

Turbulence. Flight attendants walk down the aisles, checking seat-belts. John thumbs through the flight magazine, with the map of America, a big, fold-out spread, covered with lines showing all the flight routes, black webs of lines linking city to city.

San Francisco, Sausalito and Seattle

We're staying in a pensione in San Francisco. On every floor there's a sitting area and this one has two soft chairs, some old New Yorker magazines, an entire set of *Encyclopaedia Britannica*, a tasteful lamp with a dark green metal stem and a glass-panelled window that opens. The night is cool, there's a breeze blowing, the fire-escape is just outside and there's a sycamore tree just beyond it, so close I could climb into its branches.

Today was Chinatown and the City Lights Bookstore. It was also the café just two doors up, the waiter with the coffee and cream face and the wide smile, the Golden Gate Bridge, Sausalito and the Maritime Museum.

The lift here has a heavy iron grille door. The whole building is old, this is not modern, plastic, sealed-in and air-conditioned America. We start the day with a Chinese breakfast – John with a vast bowl of soup, with noodles, bean sprouts and mint – and I have barbecue chicken and rice.

A small Mexican man opens the door for me whenever I enter or leave the hotel. I say something, to make him smile or at least for his expression to change, but it does not.

We buy cartons of juice from the Chinese store – guava, apple and wintermelon, that tastes like liquid candyfloss. Just round the corner from the hotel is Haight St, famous of course, from the sixties. The psychedelic shop has a shrine to Jerry Garcia.

Old wooden trolley buses climb the unbelievably steep hills – one curvy, curling street that we drove down last night is called Crookedest Street – and you get sudden views, vistas of lights, buildings and the Golden Gate Bridge.

Floogie's Swamp Café is nearby and the Go-getter's store is on the corner of Haight and Gough. I found the psychic store on the corner of Gough and Fell, where I bought an ephemeris for the twenty-first century.

In Northampton you can get married at the 24 Store – *and* you can choose which aisle to walk down.

Ballard, Seattle

Sitting outside Lombardi's, on the corner of Market Street NW, and 22nd Avenue also NW, in Ballard, Seattle. It's overcast but warm enough to sit in a T-shirt – just. I don't mind, I'm glad it's not so hot, on account of a new crop of insect bites. The seats here are of green plastic and the tables are green metal with glass tops, the kind of glass that looks as though someone's dipped their fingertips in it before it set, or they've blown on it with a hair-dryer, so it has lots of little wave-like depressions in it.

Borders – a sense of edge, crossing, definition, a meeting and a streaming-in of something other, something different – and I'm marking time in cigarettes and stop signs and flashing DON'T WALK signs and the friendliness of people in the cafés and the diners and the images of home and the grass growing in the back yard and the thumping of the bass from the radios in passing cars. There's an area so loose and empty in me and I wonder what I might – or might not – choose to fill it with. It's swinging like tree branches in a thunder wind, it's idling like an engine waiting at a stop light, it's got sounds in it like the waves lapping the shallow beach at Fisherman's Wharf and it's got colours like the rainbow patch flung suddenly on the street sign across from Floogie's Swamp Café.

Street people sit outside the Swamp Café with cans of Seven-up and Sprite. A black girl with a skin-tight silver lurex dress and shiny silver tights walks past. So many people and I don't know any of them, nothing of their history, their dreams or the insides of their houses. I do not know how they take their silence, whether in blue Chinese bowls, or stir-fried, or with cream and sugar. Perhaps they like the radio turned on and keep it on at nights. But I do not know what they keep behind their usual friendly gestures, or the glass of iced water they put down on the counter. No gates, no borders and no boundaries. No-one has talked of how they feel, except a tall woman on Mission Street in the Mexican area. She's thin, her hair is long and loose, her dress is long and she shouts to a boy a good head shorter than herself – you mean, you want me to go with someone else? He answers quietly, not looking at her. She walks away, returns with an empty bottle twisted behind her back. There's more shouting but we're too far away now, to hear. Later, I see a policeman talking to them both, waving his finger first at one and then the other.

A black guy walks past us, wearing earphones and he shouts – Free higher education for everyone! Sometimes I feel like shouting out too, to no-one in particular, just like the black guy walking down Mission, ears closed to the traffic noise, telling everybody what he wants to say.

The black couple in Sausalito, walking along by the water-side, choked with boats.

Are you gonna marry me? she says.

We're sitting on a bench and they're right in front of us.

Did you hear that? he says, looking at us, and again – Did you hear that? Should I run now, or later?

And of course we all smile but as they walk away it seems to me she isn't smiling or talking and I realise she was not happy about this being turned into a joke and I want to say to her – look to your own life girl, don't look to him because he'll let you down and it won't be anything to do with you and it won't be anything to do with his fault either, it's just the way it is, same as the way those boats are floating on the water, you could try all the persuading that you like, but it wouldn't get them to go underwater, it's natural for them to stay a-bobbing on the water, it isn't that they are not open to persuasion, it's just something in them that they cannot.

So what's this something lady? How are you going to say to me and make me believe that boats cannot get married? And the answer is, I cannot. For it isn't about going underwater or even about getting married. It's if you look too much to someone else, your life gets pushed to one side, your life gets skewed and it's that loss you feel, whatever or whoever you imagine might have caused it. Whatever caused it, surely is not so important as getting it back on course or even getting it back. Because that's what you want, just as the boat wants to stay floating on the water, rather than sinking.

If you go ahead and do just what you want, chances are he'll be begging you to marry him – and if he isn't, it'll most likely be because someone else has beat him to it. And at that point you may well decide to turn all offers down and follow your own course, out from Sausalito's harbour, out from the bay, out into the ocean and head north to Puget Sound if that's your choice or wherever a brisk wind and a light heart chance to take you. Life's a good journey and the last thing that you need is to be anchored before you've hardly begun.

Yesterday I was a bit sorry for myself, life-corners a little hanging down, down at heel, down in the mouth, hang dog hang, no gravy train this side of heaven, just an edge of the cold and lonelies running past my eye. But today, life is a good journey, today, we saw Mount Saint Helens, snow-capped, with a bite out of the top, that hungry sky again gone and chewed the top off Mount Saint Helens – and we come down through light cloud-smog over the city of the angels, there was a straight line there, below the blue, and when the plane came down it was through a murky mist. When we landed, the sun was shining, not too hot but pleasant and I realise this is the first hot day without bites itching me and John Chelew meets us and talks and talks and we go to a Mexican and I have tortillas with cheese and beans.

The waitress says there's no guacamole, the avocados didn't arrive this morning, so what can they do? And after our food arrives, another waitress brings us guacamole and John Chelew says, I thought there wasn't any, the other waitress said there wasn't any, and the one who brought it said 'oh' and walked away and we all looked at each other and burst out laughing.

But after that, John had to go to play in a radio show and when he got back, had to change his strings and then someone else phones up for a telephone interview and he only has time for a quick bath and no siesta at all and we'll have to be up at five in the morning, two more plane journeys, another gig, and as he walks through the courtyard of the Travelodge, to the gate, he looks tired and forlorn and my heart goes out to him.

Marcus, the sound man in Seattle at the Backstage Theatre, said he's been to Arizona and New Mexico and felt it was an ancient, ancient land, with a very specific, powerful spirit. He'd spent a night on an Indian reservation land and encountered fear the likes of which he's never known before or since.

Dreams in Chattanooga and Pennsylvania

Old Northcut Road, Turnip Town, Fannin County, Toccoa River, Chickamanga.

We're at Lookout Mountain, close to Chattanooga. The Chattanooga Choo-Choo song reminds me of my dad because he used to sing it or I have a memory of him singing it anyway, doing little skip-dances to the tune as he sang and so I remember him being light-hearted and I don't have many memories like that and it makes me cry.

Now, there is a breeze blowing through the trees just outside and an old frog is making a muted tone sound out, like someone snoring slightly. John is disenchanted because he feels this place, Lookout Mountain, is too touristy, but I think he's tired from driving all day. He wanted to find a 'perfect' place to stay for the three days off we have between gigs, but I don't know if such a place exists. Maybe it does and we'll find it tomorrow.

I dream about going to the Bessie Smith museum with my Dad. The Chattanooga Choo-Choo, the old railway station, is now a Holiday Inn.

I remember the taxi driver in Santa Monica, taking us to the airport at 5 a.m. He'd been working for twelve hours. Gee I'm tired, he says. Confidence plummets, insecurity is rife. Can he do it, can he get us there in time? I sure could do with a coffee, he says. Oh, stop for a coffee, says John. We've got plenty of time. The strange darkness of Santa Monica, where the sky isn't really dark because of all the street lights, yet it's obviously not daylight yet.

The rain, big, thick splattering drops soaking the windscreen, and in places, turning the road into a river. Steam rising from the road and the trees. One road, dark and smooth, John describes as like riding on the back of a whale.

Breakfast at the Waffle House, with grits scattered (with onions) smothered (with cheese) sliced (with chillies) and diced (with tomatoes).

New York, New Jersey, Rhode Island

Lake Hopatoong, Lake Shawnee, Lake Mohawk, New Jersey Turnpike – well, we all know about that one, from the song. It's busy, dirty, sweaty and hot, 'congested and dysfunctional' as the Interstate 285 around Atlanta was described, in a newspaper. Entrance to the Interstate 287 West this morning was also so. Roadworks meant only one lane was operating, after the toll booths.

Driving towards Sparta, New Jersey, it's just begun to rain. I mean real rain, Georgia rain, southern rain. Somewhere between Nyack and Suffering (Suffern) we stop at a Barnes and Noble bookstore and I get a bargain book – *American Women Poets*.

Sparta – Everything here is artificial, John says. Fake. Genuine fake Tudor houses, artificial water, kosherified.

It's a small plane from Newark to Providence, Rhode Island. A bus from the long-term car park, where we left the rented car, to the terminal. Not the mono-rail this time, which we got on after our arrival here, to get to the National Car Rental. Then to gate 34 and bus to the plane. I'm thinking of the garden at home, cutting the grass, sitting out in the sun. John's thinking of doing up the smiddy, clearing it out, and getting wood to floor it. I'm also thinking of old DP (Druid Prince – a character in a novel I'm writing) and how I left him and quite what's supposed to happen in this last crucial part.

The plane makes a growling sound as we taxi along. The heat as we went up the few steps to board, was immense. Not just heat from the sun, it felt like hot air from a furnace blasting at us. The metal handrail was too hot to touch. The air-conditioning doesn't seem to be working on the plane, it's very hot.

In the porch-garden area behind Stefan Grossman's house, there's a bird table and I saw a bright orange bird fly around. Yesterday I saw a rat-like creature – with stripes of yellow, black and orange, disappear into its hole in the ground. This morning, a short-tailed squirrel.

The little plane takes off easily enough, but it bumps around a bit, giving you that sinking feeling in the stomach. The 'snacks' this afternoon sound like goldfish and pratnels.

The taxi-driver in Santa Monica said – It's not so hot, I don't suppose it will be so hot in the south, but there can be a lot of humility. He was going to Las Vegas for his holiday – would he gamble? Oh, maybe a little, just a little.

Bethlehem, Pennsylvania

When I asked Stefan if he still toured much, he said that he did not. He said he was playing once – I think with John – at McCabe's in Santa Monica and he'd had a hamburger from McDonald's. You know how you don't eat very well on tour, he said, and maybe it was that – but he realised that he was just going through the set mechanically, he was not enjoying it any more and he actually walked off. And that was that. Maybe he toured a bit after that, but that was his realisation, that it was mechanical and no longer something he wanted to do.

An easy little flight today from Providence back to Newark. But not enough sleep, so we were tired by the time we arrived here in Bethlehem. We parked in a tree-shaded square off the busy East 4th Street and pushed the seats back and fell asleep. Opposite us was the porch of a house, piled with various boxes, junk and a couple of mattresses. A faint breeze came in through the open car windows. The breeze also makes the shadows cast by the leaves and branches, move and shiver. I dream that I have to move out into space, in something like the monorail at Newark airport, which arches outside of the main building, on its own little curved, enclosed and see-through metal trajectory. But mine is quite individual, quite solo, like a little bubble going out into space. Darkness. It was night. But this was a place that was mine and in the dream, time was transposed into space and therefore could be reached again, through this solo monorail trajectory, going out into the darkness.

I would go and I would come back but it was like saying to myself, I left something at home in Scotland, so I'll just pop back and get it, then come back here (to the USA). It seemed a long way to go for something, but space concertina'd into the briefest of time, and it was not something tangible I was going back to get, but more to touch base, reacquaint myself with a reference-point, that held something of identity in it.

This part of the country – the east coast – feels much more familiar and 'at home'. I wonder just how much of the strange feelings that come up have to do with the local spirits, the spirits of land, terrain, spirits of place. If you think of it, it's quite absurd to imagine that we can blithely trip through foreign terrains, with the known part of ourselves, our familiar things – clothes, books, guitar, a few possessions we can claim as our own – and think that we will arrive unchanged at every destination, that in every place we come to, regardless of the changing landscapes, the different names, streets, people and history, we will still be exactly the same.

So, we are in East 4th Street today, yesterday we were in Broad Street, Central Falls, the day before, at Long Valley, which is too small even to have streets, I think. Here, we have red brick, clapboard, we see the oddest-looking churches, with the outsides looking like crazy-paving paths – different coloured and shaped stonework, with cement joins in between. But it does not look quite real. It looks like imitation, imitating stonework that's been seen somewhere else, it looks false, ersatz, a copy, it looks painted on. It looks like a film-set, artificial. It has a blinking quality to it, an is this a dream or for real or what? quality, a dislocation, a sense of not quite knowing what is real and what is just pretend, like that familiar feeling of waking up and not knowing where on earth you are.

Especially when you wake up in a shady square in Bethlehem after going on a solo trip in a monorail bubble in darkness, far out into space where space has also become time and the sun has shifted so that the shadows of the broad-leaved trees have moved from one side of your body to the other and there is still this soft breeze blowing through the open window and the low hoot of an approaching train.

Newark airport

Yesterday was Columbia Folk Festival. South from Bethlehem, to Reading, then Lancaster. Stony Battery Road, Old Druid Hill, were road names on the way. An Amish community nearby, sign for Amityville. At the Festival, I sat in the air-conditioned trailer provided for us, eating shoo-fly pie.

I remember stumbling around on the 4th floor of the Ramada Inn near Ballard, Seattle, where there's scaffolding and boards and no proper balcony and the room numbers run out, just where our room should be. We trundle the big trolley up and down the boards. Finally, going back through the hotel and approaching from the other side, I come to the mysterious, unmarked room which has to be ours. The key fits.

To John's delight, Ramblin' Jack Elliot was playing. In between songs he talks away. He says that when musicians get together they don't talk about music, they talk about motel rooms, and the best way to get from A to B – from Scunthorpe to Birmingham – I remember him saying.

There was just a slight haze in the air when we left Columbia – it was still hot. But the haze got more and more thick and cloudy as we headed east and by the time we reached Newark it was completely grey and overcast.

We turn off at the last possible exit before the airport, to fill the car with petrol. We find ourselves in a poor area where the houses are run-down, some of them are boarded up, the streets are covered with trash, and the people sitting outside houses watch us closely as we drive by.

*

Home – such silence. The hum of the fridge. The scent from the back garden as you open the door. No more aeroplanes. I can't sleep. I've piled black avocados and green apples in the fruit bowl, put away the shopping, washed the dishes. Keep checking a streak of pale blue in the sky.

Mould in cups. Run them under the tap and there's a faint cloud around them, like steam.

The hot pastrami sandwich at the Jewish deli in Lebanon, Pennsylvania.

You talk funny, the guy says to John as we're leaving. Are you from round here? Cashew nuts and corridors in airports, long corridors and trolleys. Walkways, buses and the monorail at Newark.

Heathrow and the last plane. Finding the car in the car park at Glasgow. Remembering parking next to trees. Remembering some old life, pick it up and put it on and be very glad to be home.

11

Rome, Clusone and Remembering Giancarlo

Paolo and Stefano meet us at the airport, and we drive into Rome, past dazzling cupolas, past the sycamore-lined street beside the Tevere, past the Castel Sant' Angelo with its bridge lined with angels, past the Colosseo and then turn off into the little via Frangipani and head for the Folkstudio, where Giancarlo Cesaroni organises concerts and where John will be playing.

In the evening, walking along this street, the cobblestones are damp with rain and they gleam faintly from the light cast by the street lamps shaped like lanterns, built into the walls and leaning out at a slight angle. The metal sewer covers are embossed with the letters SPQR, which I remember learning in school. *Senatus Populusque Romanus* – the Senate and the Roman people – dates back to that far-off time of Empire and Caesars, reminds me of the peculiar Latin vocabulary we had to learn (*devastare*, to lay waste, made frequent appearances in the texts we had to read) and which had no connection with our twentieth century adolescent lives. Yet here it was, today, on a street in this legendary city I was visiting for the first time. It feels a little like landing in a fairytale read about long ago, a place remote in time and space, and suddenly, here I am, walking in these streets, the arch of Titus just a little way off, history in front of me, centuries I can reach out and touch.

The next day we walk in the sunshine to Trastevere, across the river. The plane trees with their scaly bark like mottled skin, are just beginning to leaf, forming patches of pale greenish blue around the branches. The Trastevere area is full of narrow little streets, orange and yellow walls. There's an intimate atmosphere to the place, reminding me of Florence, or parts of Paris.

Later, Paolo takes us to see the *chiesa francesi,* with the three Caravaggios in a small alcove at the back. They are practically invisible, but to get the lights to come on, so that you can see them, you have to place a coin in a slot. Paolo says he only just discovered these paintings a few days ago.

In the via Sant Eustaccio, there is a mosaic of a deer in the entrance to the café. The coffee here is particularly famous apparently. You queue up to pay and get the ticket, then you queue to get served with the coffee and even a *café grande* is quite small, comes already sugared; you then stand for about three seconds while you drink it, and it goes straight to the nerve centres, injecting animation so that you dance about like the Mickey and Minnie mouse figures dancing beside tape recorders, that various street vendors try to sell. They stand lining the via dei Fori Imperiali and in the piazza Venezia, in front of the florid building known as the *machina a scribere*, trying to sell these dancing figures made of cardboard with wool legs and a variety of other garish-coloured souvenirs, as well as watches, baseball caps and sunglasses.

Near the piazza Sant Eustaccio is a small fountain, also with a stone carved deer's head on its surface, the symbol of the deer being sacred to Sant Eustaccio. The fountain is small and unobtrusive and set in the wall.

Paolo then takes us to the church of Santa Maria degli Angeli, near Termini station. There's a pinhole of light where wall becomes roof and sunlight falls onto a spot on the floor. The spot moves as the sun moves across the sky. There's a long black line on the floor, close to and parallel with, the spot of sunlight. On either side of this line, there are exquisite marble mosaics of the zodiac signs – bull, lion, twins, crab. I want to take pictures, but a man rushes up, flapping his arms – *chiuso, chiuso,* he says. The church was built about the 4th century AD. At the time when it was built the spot of light would have fallen along the line, but now it has moved to one side – presumably because of the precession of the equinoxes.

Clusone's church bells and the Vestone angel

Here in Clusone, in the north of Italy, all the buildings are very old – the square with its astrological clock, the church with murals on the outside walls. These murals show several skeletons which I take to be people filing up to enter death or the next world – while others are being prodded by a three-pronged fork into a gaping pit. The mural is grandly titled *triompho del morte*.

It seems to me that Christianity is a dualist religion, with its good and evil, its heaven and hell. How could it not reflect the polarity of the times? Its depictions seem simplistic to us perhaps. I reject such deep divisions, not because they do not exist, both in people's ideas and experience, but because I want to go further, go beyond the dualities. Haven't we spent enough centuries being buffeted by these polarities, dividing the world up into good and bad? I think so.

Frothy cappuccinos, steep little cobbled streets, painted walls, little arches and *l'orlogio* that has the astrological symbols round it, and marks when the sun enters a new zodiac sign. The innermost circle shows the aspects.

I find a shop that sells notebooks whose covers are made of Chinese pagoda-patterned cloth. It also sells 'erotic sponges', phallus-shaped – not exactly erotic, at least not in my opinion – and glow-in-the-dark condoms.

We are high up in the mountains here and it is chilly in the morning. Scarves of mist trail half way up the steep slopes. The sun came out briefly, but has disappeared again.

*

There are two kinds of cheese on the table. One is *bel paese* and the other, whose name I do not know, has a thick rind. The rind has the colours of stone walls – grey, white, orange, seen through a window pane blurred with rain. Freckled colours of lichen and stone – a painted wall, with the colours pushed to one side or smudged in the attempt. Colours with a comb drawn through, colours seen at high-speed, losing

shape and form, turning them into lines, then the picture
frozen, with score-marks through it.

Peals of bells, long and slow, echo from the church-tower
on top of the hill, unwinding time. Playing it and reeling it
back. A clear world, of sunlight and mountains with sharp,
jagged-teeth edges, frilled with light snow, thin tucks and
seams of snow, light painted onto the mountain seams. And
further down, the bunches of pine trees and patches of green
and little red and cream nuggets of houses.

This is a world unfolding in me, like a tight wad of
paper opening out, and letting everything else fall down
the mountainside. Its unfolding creates space and peace.
It's only later that I remember what has fallen away – old

receipts and train tickets, biscuit wrappers, biros that look as if they should work, but do not. Assorted piles of papers claiming tenuous links with purposeful existence – calendars and diaries and the green blinking light of the fax machine. A complicated sense of urgency and fitting in – actions, thoughts, emotions and decisions, slotted into patterns that fan out and extend beyond the moment – that are predictable and prearranged and undeviating as tramline tracks.

Well, all these things and many others that I can't remember now, slip down the mountainsides, with the unfolding of this bunched-up thing inside me, spreading it like a scent of damp earth in the spring, or beeswax inside the stone walls of a church. Or the heavy rungs of sound from a bell-tower. They still time. Wiping it clean like a damp cloth, revealing a shiny surface. Shiny with sound or scent. They still time. And it pauses. It lets itself be swallowed by the moment. It has disappeared. And in its place there are two drifting wings. And these are the only things that you consist of. A fan of wings, swinging gates opening on this world. Bell notes, earth smells and the scent of flowers.

With time stilled, it disappears. We only know of its existence through movement, inducing a lingering sense of incompletion. A something missing feeling.

We accumulate movement, pick up speed. In cars, on trains and on the motorways, the road fans into lanes going in different directions – Milano, Bergamo, Varese, Allessandria, Sesto Calende. We stop at the toll booths, collect tickets, pay money, drive away and pick up speed. The cars weave in and out of lanes. At traffic lights, people try to sell flowers, wash windscreens, or simply ask for money. Shiny, polished tower-blocks stand sentinel by the side of the road. Blinking neon signs. The Lindt chocolate factory. Where the best-chocolate-ever is made.

It has started to rain and the sienna roof tiles are coated with silver. Yesterday, around this time, there was a thunderstorm. The air flashed bright and yellow and then God rolled his wheels across the floor of heaven. Wooden floors I guess it has. Perhaps he rolls them as children used to do, with hoops. The noise of it suggests something deeply serious, formidable, but I'm sure he must be doing it for fun. Out of sheer high spirits. The rain pummels the corrugated metal roof of a nearby building annexe. The round yellow cement mixer has stopped turning. The workmen have vanished. A wheelbarrow and bags of cement are under the protective awning. The building opposite has brown shutters on the windows and where they are open, you can see lace curtains inside the closed windows. The cobbled street outside winds steeply uphill, the beginning of the long path to the *Fontanina del Mama*, way up in the hills, where the road turns into a track and then a narrow path.

The shrine is cut into the rock, and securely behind bars. Our Lady is pale pink and blue, with reverential, folded hands. Inside the grotto there are also photos of various Popes, and tinselly offerings, hearts wrapped in plastic, faded ribbons. Hand-written pieces of paper, under stones. The writing mostly obliterated by rain. Red cylindrical candles, dedicated to St. Francis. On the path up to the shrine, there are twelve tall crosses.

*

Outside the bathroom window there are rooftops, just across a narrow street, almost close enough to touch. Their tiles are orange, yellow, grey and cream, with splashes of grey-green lichen and bright green moss folded into the edges.

The midday bell-pealing follows no kind of pattern that I can tell, it's just a rolling around sound, like water over stones, not fitted into any form, and when it gets fainter, dies away, it sounds as though it's receding into distance.

Yesterday's journey was to Vestone, via Breschia. We passed lakesides and islands, elegant castles and churches on hilltops. In the town of Vestone there's a statue of an angel, with an eagle perched on her wings. She looks strong, this angel, but she is not really here, not in this world. She is somewhere between the two, hers and ours, as close perhaps, as an angel can get to knowing what life on earth is like. Her eyes see her own world, she is not really here with us. And this eagle, it has wings of its own and I am not sure if it is a burden to her or something that is lending its strength to her, it's difficult to say, for her arms are upraised and she is holding onto the eagle's legs, which are behind her head, his feet on the curving crest of her wings. Angel assisted or burdened, it is hard to tell, but then it often is, with angels.

She is strong, but you feel it is a strength that angels should not be asked to possess, wandering outside the bounds of their dominion. I decide that the eagle is going to help her, lift her up to some more exalted realm, because this angel, she has seen too much.

The pale sun has slipped a shaky shadow on the yellow-ochre wall of the building opposite. It curves round shutters, elegantly displaced. A woman waters plants, on a balcony. Even the chimney stacks are not left alone and exposed to the sky. They have their own little roofs and their own tiles, little gestures of protection.

Rome, with its crowds of tourists and warm afternoon sun, seems a world away. The Fontana de Trevi, the Campo

Fiori with its statue of Giordano Bruno and its lopsided buildings with bits missing, giving them a slightly haunted air. All these bustling, crowded, noisy streets and now this near-silence, just the occasional rumbles of a car and the chatter of birds, a murmur of voices outside.

A silver-haired old lady, with a bright stripey cardigan, a bibbed pinafore, grey stockings and red slippers, gesticulates to a workman who has appeared under the awning, by the cement mixer. Language ripples through people's bodies here, eventually being tossed into the air, via the fingertips. Language cruises through these narrow streets, jumps, scatters and sheds sparks. It wraps itself round pillars and archways and settles smugly into the old murals, half-effaced, on the walls of the leaning buildings. Mainly the colours of dark orange and maroon remain. I cannot imagine what kind of paint they used, for it to last for centuries. Time is plastered in rich colours on these buildings. This is the real voice of the past, where the stories come from, where the tossed-away language has jumped and raced and landed on, where the language has come to rest.

Remembering Giancarlo

Mr Coeli, I said, circling the name with blue ink, that's the one. John laughed, half in disbelief, half with delight, and I handed the paper to Giancarlo, who looked at it, smiling. He looked at it with an expression of innocence on his face, amusement, interest and enjoyment. He didn't look sardonic or superior or merely calculating, as many people might have done, when informed by an utter novice at horse racing that this horse was going to win. He looked intrigued, he smiled, and I'm sure he was also looking at form and odds and history and the other things that people who like to put bets on horses look at, but he was not dismissive, for though of course he liked to win, this was also fun for him, it was a game, and one to be enjoyed.

We'd met up with Giancarlo near the Folkstudio, the tiny club in the via Frangipani in Rome, that Giancarlo had run for years now, bringing music from all parts of the world. We'd stepped cautiously into his little white *deux chevaux* Citroën. One of the doors was held onto the body of the car with grey duct tape. Another door was dented and scraped. String dangled from one of the windscreen wipers. The car rocked noticeably when John sat down in the front seat, so I sat in the back at the other side to distribute the weight. We were going to the horse races in Rome. We drove along the old via Appia, past the Circeo Massimo, bordered with the umbrella pines. The sun was shining and it was a warm spring day. I'd never put a bet on a horse in my life and had no intention of trying to use the logical approach of calculating odds. So I looked at what name had energy, what name jumped out at me and it was Mr Coeli.

Giancarlo entered into the spirit of the game and backed this horse despite its high odds and rather poor record. As did I of course. And by some fluke Mr Coeli romped in first. After that Giancarlo consulted me before putting on his bets and we all did rather well on my beginner's luck.

In the evening we went to eat at a restaurant. Giancarlo was an unassuming man, who smiled a lot. He spoke good English but with a strong Italian accent so that his English sounded as lyrical as his native language. He talked about his love of Africa and how he intended to go to live there when he retired. But he died suddenly and unexpectedly in early 1998 and so never realised that dream. What stays in my memory is his quiet, dreaming self, driving along the via Appia in his swaying, creaking car, winning at the races, eating seafood in a little restaurant, and his mentioning, in passing, how much he loved Africa, its music and its energy, its laughter and its colours and its huge blue skies.

*

I wrote *Remembering Giancarlo* after John and I drove to Edzell Castle in Scotland shortly after his death. It was still winter, the sky was grey, the trees leafless, very different from Africa or even Rome in spring. But the garden that we visited, created by Sir David Lindsay in 1601, and still preserved, retains the magic of its author's intentions, and is, so I feel, one of those special places where eternal questions relating to life and death, can be responded to. In this twilight garden, with its stone carvings of the Arts and the planetary Deities, and the topiary spelling out *Dum spiro spero*, I felt that a question had been answered. Everyone receives and translates their responses in their own way, whether through words, movement, music, colour. This was my expression of that response.

REMEMBERING GIANCARLO
(in memoriam Giancarlo Cesaroni)

He had somewhere that he loved –
I remember, as we drive through
flat country, the sky shuffling
through greys, from diffuse,
to clear, hard edges.
Grey then becomes varieties of nets
to catch the light.
From fishing-nets to fine mesh silk.

He had somewhere that he loved –
a land of blue skies, hot sun,
bright colours and dazzling music.
I remember this, as we drive
through countryside hard as a
beach shell, ridged with memories
of former life.

In some former life it seems
he was interpreter and pharmacist,
but in the one we knew
he brought music from around
the world to a tiny club
in the via Frangipani.
His face folded round his smile
like cupped hands,
dreaming of Africa.

November trees are trelliswork
and scaffolding, outlines and patterns

still to be painted, filled-in.
Waiting for summer and the real thing.

The earth is purple here
and the stone that comes from it,
pinkish-maroon.
We lose a stitch in the loops
of road round Perth,
find it again, drive through Scone
and head for Brechin.

The garden of the alchemist
is lined with plum-red stone.
The sky is apple-thick,
with a plume of elderberry.
Stone carvings line the walls –
Sol and Luna, Musica and Geometria.
Hedges are trimmed into
letters – messages of hope.
Hedges that spell. Tended,
cut, shaped into Latin words.
Dum spiro spero.
I think about the gardener.
And the patience and precision
and the love.
The cold wind felt like grit
being rubbed against the skin.

He had somewhere that he loved.
Dream or hope, vision or future –
perhaps it kept him going
pushed him on or held him back,
I do not know.

The well, set in the south wall
shows a circle of light
at the bottom. If your sight
was good enough, you could see
your own face, peering over the
stone rim, looking at the water
and reflected light.

Dusk comes slowly in the garden
of the alchemist,
with its stone carved luminaries,
deities and Arts
and its coded message, in hedge-script –
Dum spiro spero,
reminding us that life and dream
life and hope and vision –
they belong together.
I'm remembering Giancarlo
and his dream of Africa
as I close the gate behind me
to the garden of
the alchemist.

12

The Closer Sky

Since those hectic touring days in the mid-1990s, John and I enjoyed more leisurely trips, like the one to Edzell Castle in the north of Scotland in 1998, shortly after Giancarlo's death.

One of life's greatest pleasures for me has been stopping en route to brew coffee on the little gas stove John always carries in the back of the van. It doesn't matter where it is, or what the weather's like – though it's preferable of course if the sun shines – they form some of my clearest memories – rummaging around in the back of the van to find mugs, coffee and spoons among the dirty rags, hats (woolly, straw, tweed caps, felt fedoras) dishcloths, cutlery, hessian bags stuffed with indescribable pieces of cloth and chinaware – mainly blue of course – and paper bags all stuck together, whose contents might once have been sugar. But usually there was a collection of those individual little packets of sugar that John always picked up from cafés. It was as if he feared a sugar famine in the future. I learned the habit from him so that there was always sugar for his coffee when he came to visit. Another source of delight for John was coffee pots or coffee makers. The one that travelled in the back of the van was a small percolator with a glass top.

Probably the best-ever memories of the joy of coffee making and drinking in the back of the van are from the journey to Crete we made in 2013. In the morning at a small lay-by near Ancona, in the afternoon at Bari ferry terminal, with a cold wind whipping the canvas marquee – and in the luscious early morning sunshine as we parked in a deserted bay overlooking the sea near Chania, in Crete.

En route to France, 2008

On the 7th August John and I left his 'dreaming spires' (he lives in a converted church) at 5.30 in the morning. The new upper part of his dwelling is made of clean and sweet-smelling wood, and it's on a level with the little windows divided up into three upper sections and one lower one. So you can see straight outside to the tops of the trees by the river, and over to the hills beyond. There are no sounds except for the calling of birds. This upper level has only recently been created. Before, it was simply the roof, inaccessible and only vaguely seen, the windows grimed with decades of dust, dirt, the home of deceased flies and busy spiders. But with the building of an upper level, the windows were cleaned (I helped to do this) and now you have this spectacular view out over trees, water and hills. Not just the view, but the atmosphere of peace, tranquillity, of a special refuge, which I surmise is because, when this place was a church, people's aspirations would have lifted upwards and hovered by the windows and lodged in the roof beams, settled there, high above the meanness and pettiness of Everyday.

It had rained heavily all the day before. To reach this remarkable dwelling, one has to follow a path from the road, which goes over a bridge that crosses the river, and walk several metres through tall grass. A narrow swathe of path has been cut through the grass. When we leave early the next morning, we have too many things to carry in one trip, our bags and backpacks, a guitar and sitar, so John piles them in a wheelbarrow. A few bats are out late, dart past the doorway in the grey murky dawn. The river has swollen enormously and burst its banks, turning the nearby field into a lake. The church is built on a slight elevation, but the water is very close, another metre and it would enter the 'garden', the patch of grass at the front, surrounded by a railing. A grinning little gargoyle sits on the bench in front of the church, the household guardian.

And so we begin the long drive down through the corridor of England. At first the roads are quiet and empty. The first part of the motorway goes through the Lake District, passes between huge treeless hills, deep green from the rain, and as always, gives a sense of entering a very different territory, like a ritual passageway designed to engender humility in these scrawny beetle-like beings who scud past the mountain sentinels in their buzzing metal carapaces, ignoring their beauty and sublimity, forgetful of tolls and the mind's high terraces where some ancient sense of deity might be remembered and acknowledged. Just might be, in these echoing valleys.

And the high places of passage might also be remembered with nostalgia, once you've left them behind, and entered the plains, industrial, crowded with factories and houses, rows and rows of houses, streets falling away underneath the motorway flyovers, the lanes full of traffic, on and on, an endless flow of cars. We stop at services, change drivers, and the passenger dozes. The clouds have vanished, the sun is out, it's hot, and the dreaming passenger sees rose windows of colours and brilliant patterns, behind their closed eyelids.

Arrival in France

We get a little lost in London, miss the turn-off for the South Circular. Double back, find it and eventually reach Clapham where John is leaving the sitar with a friend. He doesn't want to take it all the way to Germany, where he's giving a workshop, but he'll need it afterwards for a gig in England. The sitar is dropped off and we find our way out of London again, head for Dover. The ferry is a fast one, rather small, with two forward prows like the horns of some snail-like creature, testing the waters it's about to sail through.

Not much more than an hour later, we're in France. The roads are empty, there's an enormous vista of green fields all around and the evening sun throws long thin shadows of plane and poplar trees, over the fields. The landscape undulates, the shadows are pencils, threads, dark lines that go on and on, find the horizon and keep going. Something about these lines, the way they dip and curve with the land, the way they stretch and shiver, turn into snakes, turn over, bask in this long evening light, takes me with them, horizontal shadows grow in me too and I am stretched over the hills, the thundering motorway traffic, the narrow crowded little island left far behind. We expand into this enormous evening light, into the green waves of hills, all empty and quiet, like being released from a tormented madness, into a blessed peace. The hills dip and rise, dip and curve slightly, rained on with that special light of late evening, that seems to fold a little, to follow the landscape's curves, folds like something almost material, woven out of light with slender shadow seams.

Have you noticed, I say, how as soon as one is on the mainland of Europe, the horizon becomes much much bigger? It expands so far that you think that you can see almost to where the land ends, almost to the sea?

John has not noticed. He is about to denounce this as a perceptual illusion, I can tell by a kind of stiffness he emanates into the air around him. It's to do, I say with an air of authority, with the physical landscape, which extends or contracts our perception. On any large land mass, Europe, Asia, America, you can simply see further. On an island, it's like being in a room, you can't see further than the walls, can you? You can only see what's in front of you, you are consumed by detail, which is fine for arguing existence's finer points, for following the patterns of needlework or Fair Isle knitting designs or tattoo patterns of Pictish woad but here on the mainland, your eyes can stretch themselves, they're not confined any longer, they can extend to their full capacity and it's such a relief, like being able to stretch your body after being in a confined space.

I can tell by the air going soft, murmuring a little, turning choppy like the waves of La Manche, that John has decided not to enter into an argument that he realises cannot be won. Instead, he approaches from an oblique angle that is neither agreement nor opposition. How is it, he says, that in Cornwall the sky looks closer? Because it is closer, I say.

But there's nothing in the sky, it's empty, right? I explain that the sky is not empty, that there is an atmosphere around the earth, a blanket of soft sussurant something, that we give names to, such as oxygen, hydrogen, carbon dioxide, nitrogen etc. And that this atmosphere is closer nearer the poles (I'm not sure that this is true, but it fits my argument), so that the further north in the northern hemisphere you go, the sky is closer. Hence blue-er. (Well, that is true. Look at those pale pale southern skies, where the sky is so very far away, and the clouds as distant as memories of childhood.)

He accepts this argument.

And we drive on through the evening light, the shadows slender as the seams between thoughts, inky lines like the troughs between waves, the landscape's copperplate hand-writing.

The western sky grows pink, the cloud rafts dusty purple. We stop in Montreuil-sur-Mer, whose sea is entirely imaginary, a whiff of salt only, sliding along the banks of its green river.

Our last trip together was early in 2015, to the Duddo Stones in Northumberland, and on to the East Coast, near Bamborough.

Duddo Stone Circle, sea and sunset

Glittering ground, covered with frost. Sunshine and clear blue sky. We drive to the 'secret destination' (which is there with every journey) but this time it really is a secret to John as I've planned a surprise for him. We are nearly there, and I'm looking at the map, as we go down a narrow road. A tiny signpost says 'Tiptoe only'. You're setting this up! roars he. He often imagines that there are portals into other worlds, half stage-set, half other realities always there, waiting for the keen eye or the half-dreaming eye, to reveal them. A fairy world clearly announces itself, with diminutive signs, and elaborate stage directions. But we don't follow the sign to Tiptoe, as where we want to go is in the other direction, and about 500 metres further on we stop at the entrance to a field. I don't let him read the sign which says it takes about half an hour to reach the stone circle, for it might put him off. We set off through the fields and before we reach the end of the first one, the Duddo Stones appear on the horizon, on the top of a gentle rise of ground.

Most of the stones are deeply lined, fissured, broader at the top, narrower where they sink into the ground. Like old teeth, says John, always quick with a poetic simile. From the circle the view is as if you're looking out from one of the Cathar castles into the foothills of the Pyrenees. That other clear day several years ago when I was staying at M's house near Limoux, looking after her cat while she was away on holiday. Her neighbour took me for a drive to Quéribus, then to Peyrepertuse. At Quéribus he pointed out the village of Cucugnan, made famous by le curé de Cucugnan, a character from Alphonse Daudet's *Lettres de mon Moulin*.

It was autumn, the trees flashed in the sunlight, golden tumbled bales of fiery cloth, on the hillsides. On the rocky slopes that formed caverns with the river Aude, and the road beside it, slipping and cascading over boulders, with grey rocks leaning over the road, in deep shadow. Out into the sunlight again, then climbing the long twisting road up to Quéribus. Looking down through the arrow-slits in the walls onto the flared skirt of plain below.

This English plain is much more gentle and gradual. The view east is just one field that slopes upwards to the trees at the top, but to north, west and south the view extends, mostly flat countryside, with gentle, undulating ground, the horizon to the west edged with the triple dark buttons of the Eildon Hills.

These short indented stones could be hands folded together in prayer, narrow wrists, laced fingers. On one, the indentation is curved as if formed by rivulets of water. Had they been covered by ice, by glaciers which formed runnels, when melted? John sits down on a low stone and we gaze across the plain.

A man with two small dogs comes up the path, to the stones. I say hallo but he does not respond. After walking round the ring the man says, if you spread out a bit I could get you in all the photographs. Oh, I say, I'm sorry, do you want to take photographs? No, he says, not looking at us. We move out of the circle and the man proceeds to take photographs. I suppose we should have realised, but his rudeness was astonishing.

Two other groups of people, met on the path back, were cheerful and friendly. Back at the gate, I dig out the flask of coffee and the packet of crêpes I'd brought. Pour out the coffee and we drink out of plastic cups. Another car pulls up. The driver gets out and walks through the stile. She is a young woman, dressed in bright pink and carries a hula hoop over her shoulder. She makes a bright blaze of colour against the mud brown field.

The earth feels squeezed, twisted, wrung out, then spread across the fields, drying in the sun. There is no wind, just this deep intake of the earth's breath, a long sigh of relaxation. The little road is bordered with trees planted at regular intervals. I imagine it in summer, in leaf, forming an avenue of celebration. The trees are slender, their bark is white but I don't know what kind of trees they are. At the end of the avenue, there's a handful of houses, a long barn, no sign of life.

*

On the way to the sea, we stopped off at St Anne's church in the village of Ancroft. The church was said to be eleventh century but it had been rebuilt in the nineteenth. It had a squat Norman-looking tower with slits for arrows, a defensive looking church, looked as though it would brook no nonsense, no assaults, this church was no victim, no flunkey visionary, its faith was assertive, bold, possessive of its territory.

Later, I was very glad we had looked in, for its fierce energy must have accompanied me. Looking on the map, we headed for a small road that seemed to lead to the sea. This was after getting lost, trying to reach Lindisfarne. But if we hadn't got lost we would not have reached Ancroft and visited the church. To Cheswick we went, parked the car and headed along the narrow path through the dunes. I went ahead, the path went up and down, following the hillocks of sand, with the needle grasses leaning over the path, until I stood on top, looking down on the sea below. A cliff of sand at my feet. I ran down the cliff, ran to the sea, stood on a small rock, took a photograph and a big wave threw itself at me and soaked my jeans and boots. I shouted out loud but did not move, stood firm on the foaming rock and clicked the shutter.

I took a different route back up to the top of the cliff with its thick green and sandy coloured bristles of the dune reeds. Then, rummaging in my pockets, could not find the car keys. I could not really believe they were no longer there, but after having gone through all my pockets several times, had to accept the horrible truth. I'd somehow managed to lose the keys. I walked along the ridge, following my footsteps in the sand. Back and forth, several times. How could I find keys among these long grasses? It was like looking for the proverbial needle. It was bound to be here I had dropped them, in the unfindable undergrowth of tussocks of dry grass, some in thick clumps, some in sparse fronds, with clumps of sand round their roots, and all bent over as if newly swept aside by an oncoming wave of sand-dune. John was up on an even higher ridge, between the sea cliff and the car park. I waved and shouted I've lost the keys! He started down the steep slope, laboriously edging his way between the tussocks, with his walking stick.

I looked beyond my feet to the slide of sand leading to the beach. And slithered down again, following my imprints in the sand, running to keep my balance, running until the sand became the level beach. Covering exactly the same ground, the same sand as I'd run down before, I knew this because of the clear footprints I had left. And half way to the sea, half way to the rock I'd stood on, there were the keys, lying in the sand.

I gave thanks to the sea, the sun, Saint Anne of the Ancroft Church, and Saint Cuthbert. (He must have been here, I said to John when we were in the stone circle, even though the path named after him, the path along which he is said to have walked many times, from Melrose to Lindisfarne and back, this path does not pass this way precisely, but it wasn't far away. Wouldn't he have thought this a bit pagan, says John? Not at all, say I airily, he talked to the sea eagles on Lindisfarne, he talked to the seals and all the birds, he was a very pagan enthusiast, loved solitude, sea, all of nature.)

I scramble back up the sand cliff, onto the top, all grass covered, and over the next dune, and see John appearing over a rise. I wave the keys and shout and he shouts back before disappearing into another dip. I think that John is the best person to lose keys with because he would have laughed at it, while I wailed and bemoaned our fate, he would have teased and chortled, though also would have done something about it, he would have known what to do, while I, I would have wrung my hands, because already the sun was low in the sky and would soon set, and there would be no hope at all of finding the keys in the dark, not to mention the fact that the tide was coming in and would wash over the beach and even if they had been lying, unfound, on the sand, they would have been washed away probably, with the outgoing tide. And he is also the best person with whom to find keys, because he laughs even more, at the joy of it.

Walking back to the car, a group of men come towards us. They are dressed all in black, with black hoods over their heads covering most of their faces, and carrying things – hard to see what they are – long pointed things, wrapped. Who are these guys asks John, most sinister looking, all dressed in black, and I say not black and he insists they're wearing black and I am laughing, so happy, giving thanks still to sun and sky and the saints who have accompanied us and helped me, these salvation saints, every one of them, including saints Kosmas and Damianos, my friends with the turbans from Saint Pantelimonas Church in Cyprus, I am sure they are here too and as the men approach I decide the best way to find out what they are doing is to ask them so I do, and it turns out they are carrying cameras and tripods and they smile sweetly and with excitement and tell me that a black scoter, just one, has been sighted right here on the coast at Cheswick, and they are hoping to see it. Common scoters, they can be seen here any time, but not black ones, they're from Canada and the men think it may have got lost, lost its other black companions and has joined up with common scoters, feeling lonely, and adopting the common scoters as its group, recognising a kinship with them. I wonder if it is like wild geese who sometimes fly down among domestic geese and stay with them for a while.

And so we drove back, heading west into a sky that turned pink, and then the colour spread out across the whole sky. I was driving towards this display of light and colour, like a stage set, backlit, with bars of cloud furred at the edges with a dusky purple, slightly ruffled as if someone had swept their hand slowly along the cloud's pelt, against the lie of the fur, so that little ruffle waves remained behind. Every so often one of us would exclaim in delight at this display of light, colour, cloud and sky. On and on went the small roads, then the wider road, and the sunset.